GETTING GRILLED
BY WADE CHRISTENSEN

The First Gentleman of the State of Oklahoma

By **RONNYE PERRY SHARP** and **BOB BURKE**

Series Editor: **GINI MOORE CAMPBELL**
Associate Editor: **ERIC DABNEY**

First Gentleman Wade Christensen with Burny,
Jim Christensen, and Governor Mary Fallin.

Printed in Canada.

ISBN   978-1-938923-08-1

Library of Congress Control Number   2013944707

Designed by Nathan Dunn

UNLESS OTHERWISE NOTED, PHOTOGRAPHS AND RECIPES ARE
COURTESY OF OKLAHOMA'S FIRST FAMILY.

Getting Grilled By Wade Christensen is made possible by the generosity of the following:

Phil & Jo Albert
Atkins & Markoff
Richard A. Bell
Bill Cameron
McClure Law Office
John S. Oldfield
Joan N. Perry
Norris & Betty Price
Gary & Cheryl Prochaska
Gene Rainbolt
Shawnee Milling Company

CONTENTS

Co-Authors Bob Burke and Ronnye Perry Sharp, and First Gentleman Wade Christensen with photographer Tom Flora who provided many of the photographs for the book.

ACKNOWLEDGMENTS

Oklahomans have been credited with many firsts, including electing our first female Governor in 2010. Following Governor Mary Fallin's inauguration in 2011, our state realized another first—our first "First Gentleman." It was our desire to celebrate with a cookbook and First Gentleman Wade Christensen offered to share recipes from his family, friends, and mansion staff.

This book would not have been possible without the talents of so many. Thanks to Mark Taylor from Traditions for his exceptional style and sophistication; Tom Flora of Flora Photography, Nathan King, Kathleen Fugett, and T & R Design for their creative talents; food assistant Linda Praytor for her presentation and taste buds; Liz Wood, Robin Obert, Toni Davis, and Karen Schwartz of the Governor's Mansion staff for graciously accommodating us during this process; and to our valuable technical consultants Gaye Etheridge, Sherry Hibben, Demco Printing, Ron Henderson, and Cathy Colvin.

The generosity of Gene Rainbolt, John S. Oldfield, Phil and Jo Albert, Richard A. Bell, Norris and Betty Price, McClure Law Office, Gary and Cheryl Prochaska, Bill Cameron, Shawnee Milling Company, Joan Perry, and Atkins & Markoff ensured the production of *Getting Grilled By Wade Christensen*.

We want to thank the Oklahoma Heritage Association and Director of Publications and Education Gini Moore Campbell for taking this project on and Eric Dabney for serving as associate editor. Nathan Dunn has done an outstanding job with his conception and design of the finished product.

Indeed, "it takes a village" for every successful endeavor.

Gratefully,
Ronnye Perry Sharp & Bob Burke

THE HISTORY
OF **GRILLING** AND
BARBECUE

Grilling began in the Stone Age when humans tamed fire and cooked wild animals they killed for survival. The evolution of barbecue, or BBQ, and the backyard ritual of grilling as we know it came much later.

Pit cooking has been around for thousands of years. The Polynesians were the masters of slow, pit-cooked pork. When the Spanish explorers came to the New World, they found Native Americans preserving meat by building small, smoky fires and placing it on racks over the flames. The smoke kept insects at bay and helped in the preservation process.

The word barbecue perhaps comes from the Caribbean and entered the European languages in the form barbacoa, translated "sacred fire pit." Traditional barbacoa involved digging a hole in the ground; placing meat, usually a whole goat, in the hole; covering the meat with maguey leaves and coal; and lighting it. The cooking process took several hours.

As the Spanish introduced pigs to what became the southeastern United States, barbecue took on a different flavor. Pigs and cattle became the primary meat source for the American colonies. In the South, pigs were the meat of choice as racks used to dry the meat were replaced with pits and smoke houses. The first recorded use of the English word barbecue was in 1672 when John Lederer wrote of his travels in the American southeast. Samuel Johnson's 1756 dictionary defined barbecue as "a term for dressing a whole hog," and "a hog dressed whole." In modern times, the word

GETTING GRILLED BY WADE CHRISTENSEN

barbecue also refers to a social gathering where huge amounts of barbecued meat "and the fixin's" are served, usually outdoors.

In the South, the process of cooking meat slowly often was reserved for inferior cuts of meat left for slaves and the poor. High-end cuts of meat did not need slow cooking for reducing the toughness. Throughout the South, barbecue became an inexpensive food source. Pigs could be released to forage for themselves in forests and woodlands. When meat supplies grew scarce, these semi-wild pigs could be caught, barbecued, and eaten.

Prior to the Civil War, Southerners consumed five pounds of pork for every pound of beef they ate. When wild hogs were hunted, it became a time of celebration. The traditional Southern barbecues come from gatherings commonly called "pig-pickin's."

Each area of the South has its own specific variety of barbecue, especially the sauce. As settlers moved westward, regional variations developed. In states such as North and South Carolina, sauces vary by region. In Memphis, Tennessee, barbecue is best known for tomato- and vinegar-based sauces. In Kentucky, meat is rubbed with dry seasoning and smoked over hickory wood without sauce. In Alabama and Georgia, barbecue almost is always pork with a sweet tomato-based sauce. Pulled pork is prepared by shredding the pork after it has been barbecued.

The meat-packing history of Kansas City, Missouri, has characterized still another style of barbecue. A variety of meats is used in primarily hickory smoking with tomato-based, sweet, spicy, and tangy sauces.

Outside of the Old South, barbecue has a close association with Texas. Around the world, restaurants claim to serve "Texas barbecue." The state has produced four main styles, all with different flavors, cooking methods, ingredients, and cultural origins.

Ellsworth Zwoyer of Pennsylvania patented a design for using charcoal briquettes for grilling in 1897.

GETTING GRILLED BY WADE CHRISTENSEN

THE FOUR DISTINCT STYLES OF AMERICAN BARBECUE

Carolina-style has split into Eastern, Western, and South Carolina-style, with variations largely in the sauce: South Carolina uses a mustard sauce and Western Carolina uses a sweeter vinegar-and-tomato sauce.

Memphis barbecue is probably what most of us think of when we think of BBQ — pork ribs with a sticky sweet-and-sour tomato-based mopping sauce.

Texas, being cattle country, always had opted for beef, usually brisket, dry-rubbed and smoked over mesquite with a tomato-based sauce served on the side, almost as an afterthought.

Kansas City lies at the crossroads of BBQ nation. Fittingly you will find a little bit of everything there — beef and pork, ribs and shoulder, etc. What brings it all together is the sauce: sweet-hot, tomato-based KC barbecue sauce is a classic in its own right, and the model for most supermarket BBQ sauces.

From www.foodnetwork.com

Automobile king Henry Ford's plants created briquettes from wood scraps and sawdust from his factories. Later, E.G. Kingsford bought Ford's briquette idea and began commercial production. A popular brand of charcoal still bears his name.

After World War II, families began moving to the suburbs and lived in homes with spacious backyards. Outdoor space called for outdoor pastimes, including outdoor cooking. The forerunner of the modern grill was a shallow sheet-metal pan placed atop spindly legs. Deluxe models had small wheels. The brazier grill could cook meat and other food products with the use of charcoal, although there was little control of the heat. Brazier grills left much to be desired. Often, red-hot embers were thrust upon onlookers by gusts of wind and food sometimes was incinerated on the outside and raw on the inside.

In the early 1950s, George Stephen, a worker at the Weber Brothers Metal Spinning Company in Chicago, looked for a better way to grill. He was a dedicated backyard cook and envisioned a more efficient grilling mechanism made from the metal buoys his company produced. His original idea was to cut a metal buoy in half, install vents, add a grate to the bottom section, and use the other half of the buoy as a lid. The idea worked. The first Weber kettle grill was released in 1952 and started a revolution in outdoor cooking.

The outdoor gas grill was invented in the 1960s in Little Rock, Arkansas, by William G. Wepfer and

GETTING GRILLED BY WADE CHRISTENSEN

Melton Lancaster while working for ARKLA, the Arkansas Louisiana Gas Company. Wepfer, a graduate of the United States Naval Academy, was director of marketing, charged with finding new ways to sell natural gas to ARKLA residential customers, and therefore bought a basic charcoal grill and re-designed it in the Wepfer's garage so that natural gas provided the fuel for the grill.

Grills now come in hundreds of different styles and sizes.

Gas — Gas-fueled grills typically use propane (LP) or natural gas (CNG) as their fuel source, with gas-flame either cooking food directly or heating grilling elements which in turn radiate the heat necessary to cook food. Gas grills are available in sizes ranging from small, single steak grills up to large, industrial sized restaurant grills which are able to cook enough meat to feed a hundred or more people. The majority of gas grills follow the cart grill design concept: the grill unit itself is attached to a wheeled frame that holds the fuel tank. The wheeled frame also may support side tables and other features.

Charcoal — Charcoal grills use either charcoal briquettes or all-natural lump charcoal as their fuel source. The charcoal, when burned, will transform into embers radiating the heat necessary to cook food. There is contention among grilling enthusiasts on what type of charcoal is best for grilling. Users of charcoal briquettes emphasize the uniformity in size, burn rate, heat creation, and quality exemplified by briquettes. Users of all-natural lump charcoal emphasize the reasons they prefer it: subtle smoky aromas, high heat production, and lack of binders and fillers often present in briquettes. There are many different charcoal grill configurations. Some grills are square, round, or rectangular, some have lids while others do not, and some may or may not have a venting system for heat control.

Electric — Electric grills offer an alternative by simply plugging it in. If you live where charcoal or gas are not allowed on the terrace or deck, tabletop versions, as well as full-size models of electric grills, are available.

Grilling has even gone indoors. Although live-fire cooking is difficult indoors without heavy-duty ventilation, indoor equipment can simulate some of the effects of cooking over a live fire. The simplest design is known as a grill pan, a type of heavy frying pan with raised grill lines to hold the food off the bottom of the pan and allow drippings to run off.

GETTING GRILLED BY WADE CHRISTENSEN

THE BASICS OF GRILLING

1 Know the Equipment — You may think that buying grilling equipment would be a simple enough decision. However, when you walk into a store, you will find that there is an amazing variety of grills in the market today to suit the need of every person.

From small grills designed for apartments to big covered cookers that can cater to large groups, you can find every type of grill in local stores. You will need to understand your requirements thoroughly before you shop so that you can buy a grill that is right for you and your grilling needs.

2 Know the Techniques — Most recipes will tell you which ingredients to use and how best to use them to make a great meal. Not many will tell you how to get them right on a grill. To grill anything just right, you need to get the combination of time, temperature, and taste right too. You need to know the right way of starting a fire, regulating it well, and then grilling food to just the right extent. Grilling is not the only technique; many prefer barbecuing or even smoking to bring out the real taste of meat.

3 Know the Ingredients and Flavors — Recipes can tell you in what measures you use different ingredients and what courses go well together. Some try to educate you on why a certain combination works well and which ingredients add a special flavor to your meal. Only when you know and understand the role that each ingredient plays, the special flavors that each one brings and how they all work together to create a unique dish, will you be able to work magic with your grilling.

From www.outdoorgrillingkings.com.

THE GLOSSARY OF BARBECUE

BARBECUE: Also known as barbeque, BBQ, barby, barbie, 'que, bar-b-cue, bar-b-que, and bar-B-Q, this is either a grill, a get together with an outdoor meal, or the act of cooking with a grill.

BARBECUE SAUCE: A red, yellow, or brown sauce which can be sweet, tart, spicy, or aromatic. Most are ketchup based and can be served with the food, used as a marinade, or for basting.

BASTE: To brush a seasoned liquid on to your food while it grills, to add flavor and moisture.

BROCHETTE: The French term for kabob or any food cooked on a skewer.

BULLET: A drum-shaped cooker with a dome lid. Bullets usually are cheap and made from lightweight metal.

CERAMIC BRIQUETTES: Radiant materials compressed into a brick shape and used in gas grills. They do not burn completely like charcoal. Similar alternatives are metal plates and lava rocks.

CHARCOAL BRIQUETTES: Compacted coal dust, starch, and ground charcoal used to fuel a charcoal grill.

CHARCOAL GRATE: The rack in the firebox where the charcoal goes.

CHARCOAL GRILL: A grill that uses charcoal briquettes as its main fuel.

CHIMNEY STARTER: A metal cylinder, which holds fire-starting hot coals.

DIRECT GRILLING: A way to quickly cook food by placing it on the grill rack directly over the heat. Food is often cooked covered on a gas grill but uncovered on a charcoal grill.

DRIP PAN: A foil or metal pan, which goes underneath the grilling food to catch drips.

DROP-IN GRILL: An outdoor built-in grill, which can be installed or "dropped" in an accompanying metal cart.

DRY SMOKING: Cooking food on the grill rack indirectly over the heat with the lid down. Having the vents adjusted lets the fire burn and produce smoke.

ELECTRIC GRILL: A grill powered by electricity without

an open flame. These can be used indoors as well as outdoors and are more environmentally friendly than charcoal or gas grills.

FIREBOX: The bottom of the grill, which holds the heat or fire.

FLARE-UPS: The flames produced when fat drips on to lava rocks or hot coals.

GAS GRILL: A grill that uses a natural gas line or gas from a tank as fuel.

GLAZE: To make a tasty, glossy coating on food as it cooks. A glaze is usually made by basting.

GRIDDLE: A flat piece of steel heated from beneath. Food cooked on a griddle often is called "grilled" although strictly it is griddled not grilled. These are popular in cafes and restaurants because you can use them indoors.

GRILL: Also known as a brazier, a grill is where the food sits on a grate over the flame. Grilling usually is done at a temperature of 300 degrees F or higher and some grills can reach 600 degrees F.

GRILL BASKET: A hinged wire basket that can hold foods while they grill.

GRILL RACK: Also known as a grid or grill grate, this is a latticework of metal rods which hold food on the grill.

GRILL TOPPER: A porcelain-coated grate with small holes on it which goes over the grill rack when you cook small foods such as sliced vegetables.

GRILL WOK: A wok especially made for the grill with numerous small holes and sloped sides to make grilling seafood or chopped meat or vegetables easy.

INDIRECT GRILLING: Grilling something slowly over a drip pan in a covered grill, to one side of the heat source.

KABOBS: Pieces of meat, poultry, fish, and/or vegetables, threaded on skewers and grilled.

KETTLE GRILL: A round charcoal grill, usually on three legs. These have heavy covers and can be used for indirect as well as direct grilling.

LAVA ROCK: Natural rock produced from volcanic lava, which is an alternative to ceramic briquettes in gas grills. Lava rock can be used many times but will need to be replaced eventually.

LUMP CHARCOAL: The carbon residue of charred wood in lump shapes. This is used in charcoal grills as a heat source.

MARINADE: A liquid to soak meat, fish, poultry, or vegetables in. Acidity is needed to ensure it soaks into the food and this is found in wine, vinegar, and most fruit juices.

MARINATE: To steep food in a marinade before it cooks. Marinades tenderize meat and add flavor to meat, fish, poultry, or vegetables before grilling them.

MEDIUM RARE DONENESS: The center of the meat should be bright red and the meat will be slightly springy when you press it. Medium rare is not recommended for pork, ground meats, or veal.

MEDIUM DONENESS: The center of the meat should have a pinkish red color and the meat will be springy and slightly firm when you press it.

MEDIUM WELL DONENESS: The center of the meat should have very little pink and the meat will be firm and springy when you press it.

PORTABLE GRILL: A small camping style grill with a push button ignition.

ROTISSERIE: The long metal skewer or spit that suspends and rotates food over the heat source of the grill.

RUB: A blend of seasonings rubbed over the food before grilling.

SEARING: Cooking meat over a high heat for a short time to create a crunchy outer surface. It is a myth that searing seals in the juices.

SIDE BURNER: A burner on the side of the grill for non-grill cooking.

SKEWER: A long, thin wooden or metal stick inserted through meat, poultry, fish, or vegetable pieces for grilling.

SMOKER BOX: A perforated metal box which goes on the briquettes or lava rocks of a gas grill or on the grill rack of a charcoal grill to hold wood chips and release smoke.

SPICES: Powder made from dried bark, berries, seeds, roots, or pods. Used to add flavor to grilled foods.

THERMOSTAT: A device for measuring temperature and regulating heat.

TUNING A PIT: Modifying a cooker for good, even smoke and heat distribution.

VENTS: Holes in a firebox or grill cover. The air circulates through open vents to increase a fire's heat.

WATER SMOKERS: A water pan close to the heat source. The moisture evaporates, keeping the humidity high. You can use beer, wine, juice, celery, herbs, and more in the water pan and the resulting steam flavors the food.

WHITEBONE: What happens if you cook ribs too long? If you pull on two adjacent ribs and the meat falls off one rib, exposing the bone, it is overcooked.

WOODCHIPS AND CHUNKS: Natural wood added to a fire to give a smoky flavor to the food while it cooks. Apple, alder, hickory, cherry, oak, mesquite, pecan, and maple are popular. These woodchips are soaked in water, drained, and then added to the fire just before putting on the food.

OKLAHOMA'S FIRST
First GENTLEMAN

The title of First Gentleman of Oklahoma was born in January, 2011, when Mary Fallin was inaugurated as the state's first woman governor. The spouses of Oklahoma's 26 previous male governors were officially known as the First Lady of Oklahoma.

Wade Christensen, Governor Fallin's husband, is a fourth-generation Oklahoman with deep roots in the pioneer farming and ranching heritage of western Oklahoma. His great grandparents came from Denmark and Tennessee in the late 1800s and began farming near Thomas in Custer County long before the Great Depression and dust storms drove many farmers from the land.

The succeeding generations of Christensens stayed with the land and, through hard work and dedication, accumulated sizable tracts of farmland in Custer and Blaine counties. Wade's parents, Jim and Jo Christensen, farmed the land together with Jim's brother, in the same manner that Wade's grandfather and his brothers did. They raised quality cattle and a variety of field crops that included wheat, alfalfa, milo, canola, oats, barley, mung beans, cotton, and even black-eyed peas. Wade and his siblings still farm together as his family has done for generations.

Wade's father Jim earned a triple bachelors degree from Southwestern Oklahoma State University in secondary education, business, and accounting. He earned a double major from Oklahoma State University in school administration and accounting and his professional certificate from the University of Oklahoma. He was a teacher and principal in the El Reno public school system when Wade was born in 1954. Wade's mother, likewise, earned a bachelors degree in music from Oklahoma City University and a masters degree in education from Oklahoma State University. She was an exceptional teacher and gifted organist and pianist.

On weekends, Jim worked on the family farm near Thomas. By the time Wade completed the first grade, Jim decided to return full time to farming and the family moved to a house across the section from Jim's parents one mile south of Thomas.

Wade, left, was introduced to the family kitchen at an early age. He watches his baby brother, Drew, while his mother prepares the evening meal.

The family grew as three more children were added. Drew, who obtained an accounting degree, still farms and lives in the house where Wade grew up. Clay is an attorney in Oklahoma City. Their only sister, Jane VanFossen, is an elementary teacher in the Tulsa Union public school system.

Life was busy on the Christensen farm. During the harvest season, days began early and ended late. Young Wade drove a tractor and combine long before he had a license to drive an automobile. While in grade school, Wade's mother also taught him to play the piano. From his first memories, he developed a lasting appreciation of nature and the rural way of life. He knows well the different smells after wheat and alfalfa have been cut and is still in awe of the serene beauty

Wade's mother, Jo, was an accomplished organist.

of a western Oklahoma sunrise hidden in the mist that hovers over recently-broken ground.

Wade was an active member of the 4-H Club and Future Farmers of America (FFA). He showed cattle, hogs, and horses at livestock shows and expositions. Some of his first trips outside Custer County were to 4-H Roundups in Stillwater, the State FFA Convention in Oklahoma City, and the National Convention in Kansas City, Missouri. He was a member of the National FFA Band and played the trombone. In 1973, he was named Oklahoma's Star Farmer at the FFA Convention and later was named the First Star Agri Businessman of the Western Region of the United States. He is a farmer at heart.

After graduating from Thomas High School, Wade declined a football scholarship offer from Southwestern

Oklahoma State University at Weatherford and accepted a President's Leadership Scholarship at Oklahoma State University. On the Stillwater campus, he was involved in intramural sports, various collegiate social and political student organizations, and was a member of the Sigma Nu fraternity. He earned a business degree in 1977.

The only part of life that stayed constant for Wade in his college years was his commute from Stillwater to Thomas on the weekends to help on the family farm. Most of the time he would drive, but sometimes he would fly his Cessna airplane. As part of Wade's lifelong summer farm responsibilities he often can be seen driving an 18-wheeler rig up and down the interstates pulling a combine, tractor, cattle feeder, or potbelly grain trailer. Later in life he even hauled a Caterpillar dozer to his Deer Creek home, signaling to his neighbors the start of building a new home. After graduation, he returned to Thomas and farmed for three years before enrolling in law school at the University of Tulsa where he earned a law degree in 1983. During law school, he worked part time at a Tulsa law firm and spent many weekends and summers on the family farm. Over the years Wade

The Christensens celebrated special occasions with family meals, as on grandmother Nola Christensen's birthday in 1978.

has built a successful law practice representing employers and insurance companies in claims before the Oklahoma Workers' Compensation Court. He also represents a number of other business interests, including banks, oil and gas companies, and health care companies. Active in a variety of clubs and organizations, Wade currently is the first Oklahoman to chair the National Governors Association Spouses Leadership Committee.

Even though Wade is a practicing attorney in downtown Oklahoma City, he moved his children to the country where they would have some "room to roam" as they grew up. Wade also managed to take his children back to his home town of Thomas during wheat harvest and other times during the year so they could learn some of his appreciation for rural Oklahoma farming and ranching. It always has been very important to Wade that his children learn the value and importance of the rural way of life.

Wade has four children of his own and two stepchildren. Blake is a graduate of the University of Oklahoma and the Oklahoma State College of Osteopathic Medicine. Currently he is a fourth-year anesthesiology resident at the University of Oklahoma Medical Center. Adam is a graduate of the University of Oklahoma and earned his MBA and Juris Doctorate from Oklahoma City University. Adam works in the Christensen Law Group.

Wade's third child, Brittiany, works as a veterinary technician associate and attends Oklahoma City Community College. Alex, Wade's youngest, is attending the Health and Exercise Science College at the University of Oklahoma. Christina Fallin, Wade's stepdaughter, is a University of Oklahoma graduate and is working as a professional/ consultant businesswoman. Price Fallin will graduate from the University of Oklahoma in December, 2013, with a degree in entrepreneurship and MIS.

One of Wade's finest attributes is his love for his family and the attention he gives his children as they grow up.

Wade first met Mary Fallin during their college days— but it was a casual acquaintance at best. They met again after Fallin was elected lieutenant governor of Oklahoma and a member of Congress. Occasionally, Wade and his law partner, Bruce Day, met with Fallin to talk about business and legislative affairs. At one particular luncheon meeting with Fallin in 2009, Day left early and Wade and Mary were left alone to talk for a few minutes. A few minutes turned into a few months and two rings. They found they had a lot in common—especially total involvement in the lives of their children as single parents.

Wade wanted to ask Mary to marry him in a special way, in a special place. He chose the massive Lincoln Memorial in Washington, D.C., rather than some fancy restaurant, because he believed his future wife and President Abraham Lincoln had similar values of inspiration, hope, and love for country. Wade sought the assistance of Mary's close friend, Margaret Ann Morris, to assist in his plan. Margaret Ann's role was to ask Mary to meet her and several friends at the Memorial to take a photograph. Margaret Ann was actually at home in Oklahoma City as she texted Mary, setting up a specific time for the photograph.

Meanwhile, Wade arrived in the nation's capitol in a driving rainstorm and traveled by taxi to the Lincoln

Memorial and his four-hour wait for Mary to finish voting in Congress. When security officers wondered why a man in a nice suit kept pacing in front of the huge statue of President Lincoln, Wade had to tell them his plan to make a surprise proposal to a Congresswoman. Some of the officers were so excited they stayed past the end of their shift to watch the proposal.

Mary's hectic schedule caused her time to meet Margaret Ann at the Lincoln Memorial to be pushed back. Meanwhile, Wade continued to pace—he was determined to make the moment one neither of them would ever forget. Finally, around 7:00 p.m., in near darkness, Mary left the Capitol. As she neared the Lincoln Memorial, her driver mistakenly passed the turn and she was forced to walk a block through the rain and over a soaked lawn to get to the Memorial.

For hours Wade had watched other women walk up the long steps to the Lincoln statue—only to see that it was not Mary. Finally, Mary arrived, climbed the steps, and was shocked to see Wade. She exclaimed, "Wade! Is that you?" She thought he was in Oklahoma City.

Not to lose his intended element of surprise, at the foot of President Lincoln, Wade dropped to one knee, pulled a ring from his pocket, and asked Mary to be his wife. Excited, surprised, and covered in rain, she said, "Yes!" They were married on November 21, 2009. Less than one year later, Mary was elected as the first woman governor of the State of Oklahoma.

After Mary was inaugurated as Oklahoma's 27th Governor on January 10, 2011, Wade assumed his new role as First Gentleman of Oklahoma. He and his youngest son, Alex, still a student at Deer Creek High School, moved into the governor's mansion. Later, Wade's son, Adam, also moved into one of the bedrooms in the historic home while studying for the Bar Examination. Even today there are nights when Blake, Adam, Price, and Alex hang out with each other and spend the night. "With Mary's children and my children frequenting the mansion, there is always something different happening, which is fun." Wade said.

The First Gentleman is his own man. He is in no way intimidated by the fact that his wife is the chief executive of the state. He is very proud of his wife and is honored to provide support in any way he can. His best friends of many years have seen no change in him, although he arrives at court each day escorted by one of the state troopers assigned to provide security for the Governor and his or, in this case, her spouse.

When asked if he has a "cause" as First Gentleman, Wade said, "My only cause is to promote Oklahoma. I love the land. I love being a farmer—the pride of ownership of land and the feeling of accomplishment when harvest comes. We are blessed to be in Oklahoma because here, we can do anything and do it better than in most other areas of the country."

A special gleam appears in Wade's eyes when he talks about getting up early, watching the sun rise, and walking through rich soil recently broken by a disc pulled by one of the family's tractors. To Wade, "There is nothing like the smell of fresh-tilled soil, especially after a summer shower has cooled the day and the steam rises from the ground."

OKLAHOMA'S FIRST FIRST GENTLEMAN

The Christensen family when Wade was a senior at Thomas High School. Left to right, Wade, Clay, Jane, Drew, Jo, and Jim.

Wade with his children and his father. Left to right, Brittiany, Blake, Wade, Jim, Adam, and Alex.

Oklahoma's First Gentleman is comfortable on any occasion, whether dressed in blue jeans or decked out in a tuxedo for a formal dinner.

The Governor and First Gentleman dance at the inaugural ball in January, 2011. They were married in Oklahoma City on November 21, 2009.

GETTING GRILLED BY WADE CHRISTENSEN

The Christensens at the family farm near Thomas. Left to right, Clay, Wade, Drew, and Jane. Their father, Jim, is in front.

On a combine on the Christensen farm during harvest, Wade's love for the western Oklahoma family farm has now become part of the Governor's life.

As part of his role as First Gentleman, Wade went sailing with several First Ladies at the National Governors' Conference in 2012.

The First Gentleman with the five living former Miss America pageant winners from Oklahoma. Left to right, Lauren Nelson, Susan Powell, Wade Christensen, Jane Jayroe, Shawntel Smith, and Jennifer Berry.

GETTING GRILLED BY WADE CHRISTENSEN

The First Family—Blake Christensen, Christina Fallin, Price Fallin, Governor Mary Fallin, First Gentleman Wade Christensen, Alex Christensen, Brittiany Christensen, and Adam Christensen.

GRILLING
AT THE MANSION WITH THE
FIRST FAMILY

Wade's Filet Mignon
with Sauteed Mushrooms

6 TO 8 OUNCE FILET MIGNON STEAKS
KOSHER SALT AND FRESH CRACKED BLACK PEPPER
½ TABLESPOON OF BUTTER PER STEAK
GARLIC POWDER

When I am grilling a good steak, timing is everything. I like to take my steaks out of the refrigerator and let them sit until they reach room temperature. My personal seasoning preference is fresh cracked black pepper, maybe a little garlic powder, whatever you like. Season steaks on both sides. It has always been my theory not to put salt on steaks until after you have cooked them. After I have removed my filet from the grill I place a pad of butter on each filet and let the steak rest for 2 or 3 minutes before serving. Cook steaks 9 to 10 minutes per side on medium to hot grill or less for desired doneness.

Sauteed Mushrooms

3 TABLESPOONS BUTTER

1 POUND FRESH MUSHROOMS, SLICED
(I USE WHITE OR BABY BELLA)

1 TABLESPOON DRIED MINCED ONION

¼ CUP DRY WHITE WINE

SALT AND PEPPER TO TASTE

2 TEASPOONS WORCESTERSHIRE SAUCE

I melt my butter in a large skillet adding mushrooms and saute for a few minutes, until mushrooms start to soften. Then you want to add remaining ingredients and cook uncovered over low heat for 30 minutes or until mushrooms are tender. The sauteed mushrooms complement the filet creating an exceptional taste.

Wade Christensen

GETTING GRILLED BY WADE CHRISTENSEN

Cousin Todd Morrow's Steak & Shrimp

RIBEYE, NEW YORK STRIP, OR T-BONE STEAK
MEDIUM TO LARGE SHRIMP
BUTTER
LEMON AND PEPPER SEASONING SALT
WORCESTERSHIRE SAUCE

Prepare the steaks: Tenderize the steaks, I use my fist. Place the steaks in a large ziplock bag with a generous amount of Worcestershire sauce and marinate for several hours (the longer the better).

Peel shrimp by hand, starting with the legs, and remove the shell leaving the tail. Thread the shrimp on bamboo skewers. Melt ¼ stick of butter and brush on shrimp. Sprinkle on desired amount of lemon pepper. When cooking shrimp on the grill, the less time I find is better because it's easy to overcook the shrimp. About 3 to 4 minutes on each side is probably all you'll need.

Apply desired amount of lemon pepper to the steaks. I use charcoal instead of a gas grill, just my personal preference. The key to what I think is a great flavor is adding pecan wood sticks over the prepared coals. Steak-and-shrimp is a great no-brainer, but what makes it really great is the pecan smoke. A couple sticks are good. Don't build a campfire.

I've found the key to good grilling is also paying attention to the food on the grill and not getting distracted.

Governor's Favorite Balsamic Chicken

MARINADE:

1 CUP BALSAMIC VINEGAR

1 TABLESPOON GARLIC PASTE

2 TABLESPOONS PEPPER

¼ CUP OLIVE OIL

1 TEASPOON SALT

6 BONELESS, SKINLESS CHICKEN BREASTS

Combine first five ingredients, mix well, and pour into a plastic freezer bag. Add chicken breasts and marinate for three to four hours turning often. Grill chicken breasts and enjoy!

Chef Robin L. Obert

Blake Christensen's Shrimp

¼ CUP BASIL (CHOPPED)

4 GARLIC CLOVES

¼ CUP LEMON JUICE

2 TABLESPOONS TOMATO PASTE

¼ CUP OLIVE OIL

¼ CUP WHITE WINE

1 TABLESPOON GINGER PASTE

#1 SHRIMP U20 (LARGE)

¼ CUP TOMATO (SMALL DICE)

2 TABLESPOONS GREEN ONION
(SLICED ON A DIAGONAL)

12 BASIL LEAVES (MEDIUM SIZED)

2 TABLESPOONS CAPERS

2 TABLESPOONS OLIVE OIL

3 TABLESPOONS LEMON JUICE

1 TEASPOON GARLIC PASTE

ITALIAN BAGUETTE

Combine the first seven ingredients and mix in a blender. Pour into a plastic freezer bag and add shrimp. Allow to marinate one to two hours. Grill shrimp to desired doneness.

Slice baguette and lightly brush one side with olive oil and grill until golden brown.

In a bowl combine diced tomato, green onion, garlic paste, capers, olive oil, and lemon juice until thoroughly mixed.

Top toasted baguette slices with basil leaf, tomato mixture, and finally the shrimp. Serve immediately.

Chef Robin L. Obert

Ribs for Price Fallin

MARINADE:

2 BABY BACK RIB RACKS

1 CUP YELLOW MUSTARD

½ CUP BALSAMIC VINEGAR

⅓ CUP BROWN SUGAR

2 TABLESPOONS BUTTER

1 TABLESPOON WORCESTERSHIRE

1 TABLESPOON LEMON JUICE

1 TEASPOON(OR TO TASTE) CAYENNE

½ CUP ONION (GRATED)

⅔ CUP CIDER VINEGAR

1 TABLESPOON GARLIC (GRANULATED)

TABLESPOON TO TASTE SALT AND PEPPER

RUB:

2 TABLESPOONS BROWN SUGAR

1 TABLESPOON CUMIN

¼ CUP PAPRIKA

2 TABLESPOONS BLACK PEPPER

1 TEASPOON CAYENNE

3 TABLESPOONS SUGAR

1 TEASPOON SALT

2 TABLESPOONS DRY MUSTARD

2 TEASPOONS GARLIC (GRANULATED)

2 TEASPOONS ONION (POWDERED)

Combine all ingredients for the marinade and mix well. Marinate ribs overnight.

Once marinated, lightly cover ribs with rub and smoke at 225 degrees for five or six hours (until done).

Reserve marinade and reduce to a sauce for the cooked ribs.

Chef Robin L. Obert

Quinoa Burger
for **Christina**

1 CUP QUINOA (WHITE)
    (COOKED PER PACKAGE DIRECTIONS)

½ CUP PORTOBELLA MUSHROOM
    (GILLS SCRAPED OUT AND RESERVED)

¼ CUP BLACK BEANS (PUREED)

2 TABLESPOONS RED BELL PEPPER
    (FINE DICE)

¼ CUP CHEESE BLEND (ITALIAN)

2 TABLESPOONS WHITE WINE

1 TEASPOON GARLIC

TO TASTE SALT AND PEPPER

Grill portobella and cut to fine dice. Lightly sauté red bell peppers and garlic, finish with white wine and reserved portobella gills. Remove from heat, add quinoa, and all remaining ingredients. Form into patties. Cook on medium heat in a non-stick pan to a golden brown.

Chef Robin L. Obert

Sriracha Skirt Steak over Watermelon for Alex Christensen

MARINADE:

½ CUP TERIYAKI

1 ½ TEASPOONS GARLIC PASTE

2 TEASPOONS GINGER PASTE

1 ½ CUPS WATERMELON WATER

2 TABLESPOONS SESAME OIL

2 TABLESPOONS SRIRACHA

2 TABLESPOONS GRATED ONION

2 TABLESPOONS LIME JUICE

1 TEASPOON LIME ZEST

2 TABLESPOONS HONEY

2 TABLESPOONS GRAPE SEED OIL

3 POUNDS SKIRT STEAK

WATERMELON SALAD:

3 CUPS WATERMELON (MEDIUM DICE)

2 TABLESPOONS SRIRACHA

¼ CUP RICE WINE VINEGAR

1 TABLESPOON AGAVE NECTAR

2 TABLESPOONS PABLANO PEPPER (SMALL DICE)

2 TABLESPOONS GREEN ONION

Combine ingredients for marinade and pour into a plastic freezer bag. Place skirt steak into mixture and marinate four to six hours. Grill steak to desired doneness.

Combine ingredients for watermelon salad and allow to sit in refrigerator for one hour.

Serve skirt steak over salad.

Chef Robin L. Obert

Adam Christensen's Favorite Ribs

DRY RUB:

¾ CUP PAPRIKA

2 TABLESPOONS DRY MUSTARD

¼ CUP ONION POWDER

1 TABLESPOON GINGER
  (GROUND)

1 TEASPOON CLOVE
  (GROUND)

¼ CUP PEPPER (BLACK)

1 TABLESPOON GARLIC
  (GRANULATED)

2 BABY BACK RIB RACKS

CHIPOTLE GLAZE:

4 CUPS RED WINE

4 GARLIC CLOVES (CRUSHED)

2 TABLESPOONS CHIPOTLE
  IN ADOBO

¼ CUP HONEY

Combine first seven ingredients and place in airtight container. There will be left over rub which can be stored for future use. Cover two rib racks with a liberal amount of rub, wrap with plastic wrap, and place in refrigerator for four hours or overnight. Pull ribs and bring to room temperature. Smoke at 225 degrees for five to six hours.

For the glaze combine the red wine, garlic, chipotle in adobo, and honey. Cook on medium and reduce down to syrup consistency. Do not over reduce as mixture will not pour. Check by placing a drop of the syrup on a cool plate.

Once ribs are cooked drizzle chipotle glaze over them and serve.

Chef Robin L. Obert

Great Cheese Dip

8 OUNCES SHREDDED MONTEREY JACK CHEESE
8 OUNCES SHREDDED CHEDDAR CHEESE
8 OUNCES SHREDDED MOZZARELLA CHEESE
1 TABLESPOON CHOPPED JALAPENOS
½ SMALL CAN CHOPPED GREEN CHILES
1 MEDIUM MINCED ONION
1 CUP LIGHT MAYONNAISE
SLICED OLIVES FOR GARNISH IF DESIRED

I am not sure who gave me this recipe, but it has become a family favorite. I combine all the above ingredients except the olives. Bake at 350 degrees for 25 minutes. Garnish with olives. We love to serve this dip with scoop Fritos. Serve hot.

Jane VanFossen

Wade, Clay, and Drew Poco Pepper Snacks

1 (3 OUNCE) PACKAGE OF CREAM CHEESE, SOFTENED
½ CUP SHREDDED CHEDDAR CHEESE
2 TABLESPOONS CHOPPED JALAPENOS
2 TABLESPOONS CHOPPED RIPE GREEN OLIVES
1 TEASPOON INSTANT MINCED ONION
4 DROPS HOT PEPPER SAUCE
1 CAN CRESCENT DINNER ROLLS

The brothers and I combine all ingredients except crescent rolls. Separate crescent dough into 4 rectangles. Press perforations to seal. Spread ¼ of cheese mixture over each rectangle. Roll up and seal (jelly roll fashion). Refrigerate for at least an hour. Cut each roll into 10 slices and place on greased cookie sheet. Bake for 12-14 minutes at 400 degrees. Serve hot.

Christensen Brothers

Old-Fashioned Cole Slaw

You need to let your vegetables stand for 2 hours or more. Drain them thoroughly then add your dressing mixture. Store in refrigerator.

Nola Christensen

2 LARGE HEADS CABBAGE
4 LARGE CARROTS
6 RED PEPPERS
6 GREEN PEPPERS
8 SMALL ONIONS
½ CUP SALT

DRESSING:
5 CUPS VINEGAR
4 CUPS SUGAR
3 TABLESPOONS CELERY SEED
2 TEASPOONS DRY MUSTARD

Corn Relish Dip

2 CANS MEXICAN CORN, DRAINED
1 LARGE JAR PIMENTOS
2 CANS CHOPPED GREEN CHILES
½ CUP PARMESAN CHEESE
12 OUNCES MONTEREY CHEESE, GRATED
1 CUP MAYONNAISE (REAL)

Mix together and put in 9×13 inch, greased pan. Bake at 350 degrees for 30 to 40 minutes. Eat with Fritos.

Drew Christensen

Frozen Fruit Salad

2 LARGE CONTAINERS OF
    COOL WHIP
8 OUNCES SOUR CREAM
16 OUNCES CRUSHED
    PINEAPPLE (DRAINED)
½ CUP MARASCHINO CHERRIES
1 CUP CHOPPED NUTS
1 CUP SUGAR
5 LARGE BANANAS – MASHED
    WITH 2 TABLESPOONS LEMON JUICE

Mix together and freeze in a 9×13 pan. This is a family favorite.

Jo Christensen

Confetti Salad

PACKAGE OF FIELD GREENS (OR ROMAINE LETTUCE)
PACKAGE OF BABY SPINACH
1 CHOPPED GREEN PEPPER
1 CHOPPED RED PEPPER
1 CHOPPED YELLOW PEPPER
THINLY SLICED RED ONION, AMOUNT AS DESIRED
SMALL CAN SLICED RIPE OLIVES (DRAINED)
SLICED MUSHROOMS (IF DESIRED)
PACKAGE SHREDDED PARMESAN CHEESE
PAUL NEWMAN'S BALSAMIC VINAIGRETTE DRESSING

When all the ingredients have been added to the bowl, I add about half of the bottle of the dressing (shaken well) and drizzle over the salad and mix thoroughly.

This delicious salad makes a colorful addition to a buffet meal. There is never any left!

Barb Morrow

Cherry Salad

- **1 CAN CHERRY PIE FILLING**
- **1 CAN CRUSHED PINEAPPLE (DRAINED)**
- **1 CAN MANDARIN ORANGES (DRAINED)**
- **1 LARGE CONTAINER COOL WHIP**
- **1 CAN EAGLE BRAND MILK**
- **OPTIONAL – NUTS**

This is a standard favorite of our family for any occasion. Christmas, Thanksgiving, special celebrations, even barbecues. Mix all ingredients well and chill.

Gail Christensen

Mom's Hot Rolls

- **2 PACKAGES YEAST**
- **1 TEASPOON SUGAR**
- **1 CUP LUKEWARM WATER**
- **2 CUPS MILK, SCALDED**
- **⅔ CUP MELTED SHORTENING**
- **¾ CUP SUGAR**
- **4 TEASPOONS SALT**
- **2 BEATEN EGGS**
- **10-11 CUPS SIFTED FLOUR**

Our family could never get enough of Mom's homemade rolls. They would just melt in your mouth. Soften yeast and dissolve 1 teaspoon sugar in lukewarm water. Add milk; cool to lukewarm and add shortening, sugar, and salt. Add eggs and beat well. Add flour to make soft dough. Knead lightly for 10 minutes. Place in greased bowl. Grease top of dough and cover. Let rise until double in bulk. Shape into rolls and let rise again. Bake at 375 degrees for 20 minutes.

Jo Christensen

Cinnamon Rolls

DOUGH:

1 CUP OF SUGAR

1 TEASPOON OF SALT

3 PACKAGES OF ACTIVE DRY YEAST

8 TO 9 CUPS OF ALL-PURPOSE FLOUR

2 CUPS OF WHOLE MILK

1 CUP OF BUTTER

2 EGGS

FILLING:

2 ¼ CUPS OF BUTTER

⅓ CUP OF GROUND CINNAMON TO SPRINKLE

2 ¼ CUPS OF SUGAR

HEAVY CREAM (ENOUGH TO COVER BOTTOM OF PAN)

⅓ CUP OF BROWN SUGAR

ICING:

1 POUND OF POWDERED SUGAR

1 POUND OF LIGHT BROWN SUGAR

⅓ CUP OF WHOLE MILK

1 STICK OF BUTTER

2 TABLESPOONS OF BREWED COFFEE OPTIONAL

½ CUP OF CHOPPED PECANS OPTIONAL

Start by using a large bowl and combining the sugar, salt, yeast and 2 cups of the flour. At the same time in a 2-quart saucepan, heat the milk and the butter until very warm (from about 120 degrees to 130 degrees). The butter does not have to melt. Then, with a mixer at LOW speed, gradually beat the liquid from the saucepan into the dry ingredients. After a minute or so, increase the mixer speed to MEDIUM and beat an additional 2 minutes more, occasionally stopping and scraping the bowl with a spoon or spatula. After the 2 minutes, beat in the eggs and 2 cups of flour for another two minutes or so. Don't forget to stop occasionally to scrape the bowl. After the two minutes are up, stir in enough flour (with a wooden spoon) to make a soft dough. Now, turn the dough onto a large, lightly-floured, wooden cutting board. Knead the dough until it is smooth and elastic, which should take about 10 minutes. Shape the dough into a ball. Grease a large mixing bowl with Crisco and then pour dough ball into the bowl, flip the dough over once. Now, let the dough rise in a warm and dry place for about 1 hour—it should about double in size. Finally, after the hour is up and the dough has risen, punch down the dough with your fist in the middle. Then, cover the bowl and let the dough rest for about 15 minutes. You are now ready to proceed with the preparation of the cinnamon rolls themselves.

While your dough is resting, you will need to cover the bottom of your pan with heavy cream and brown sugar. Then, in a small bowl, combine the brown sugar and cinnamon. If you plan to use the pecans add them in also. Set aside this mixture. Now, cut the roll in half and roll out the portion into an 18" by 12" rectangle. If it is shorter than 18", don't panic. Once the dough has been rolled out, pour half of the melted butter onto the dough. Brush the butter to spread it equally over the dough, making sure to brush the ends. Hand-sprinkle the sugar/cinnamon mixture onto the battered dough. Use your hand to spread the mixture to the edges of the dough. Now, starting at the 1" (long) side of the dough rectangle, roll the dough as tight as possible into a jelly-roll fashion. Pinch the end seam to seal the roll after rolling. With the roll seam-side down, cut the rolls into 1 to 1 ½ inch slices. Place them in one of the 13" by 9" pans and cover. You should let them rise for about 40 minutes. While this first batch is rising, repeat the process with the other half of the dough roll. After the first set of rolls has completed its rising, preheat your oven to 400 degrees. Place on the center rack and bake for 25 minutes or golden brown on top. Repeat the process for the next batch. Now you can cover the rolls with your special icing. It is better to pour the icing after the rolls have cooled slightly.

Drew Christensen

Squash Casserole

1 PACKAGE PEPPERIDGE FARM STUFFING MIX
1 PACKAGE STICK BUTTER
2 POUNDS YELLOW SQUASH
2 MEDIUM ONIONS
SALT TO TASTE
1 CAN CREAM OF CHICKEN SOUP
1 CAN CHOPPED WATER CHESTNUTS
1 SMALL JAR PIMENTOS
1 (8 OUNCE) SOUR CREAM
¼ POUND CHEESE, GRATED

Melt and mix butter with stuffing. Then cook squash and onions until tender. Mix soup, water, chestnuts, pimentos, and sour cream into cooked squash. Layer half of dressing mix in 9x13 inch pan. Add squash mixture. Top with ¼ pound grated cheese and remainder of dressing mix. Bake at 350 degrees for 50 minutes. Serves 8.

Mary Jo Copeland

Grilled Stuffed Portobello Mushrooms

¾ CUP CHOPPED PLUM TOMATO

½ CUP SHREDDED PART-SKIM MOZZARELLA CHEESE

1 TEASPOON OLIVE OIL, DIVIDED

½ TEASPOON FINELY CHOPPED FRESH ROSEMARY

½ TEASPOON GROUND BLACK PEPPER

1 GARLIC CLOVE, CRUSHED

4 (5-INCH) PORTOBELLO MUSHROOM CAPS

3 TABLESPOONS FRESH LEMON JUICE

2 TEASPOONS SOY SAUCE

COOKING SPRAY

2 TEASPOONS FRESH PARSLEY

Prepare grill.

Combine the tomato, cheese, ½ teaspoon oil, rosemary, pepper, and garlic in a small bowl.

Remove brown gills from the undersides of mushroom caps using a spoon and discard gills. Remove stems; discard. Combine ½ teaspoon oil, juice, and soy sauce in a small bowl; brush over both sides of mushroom caps. Place the mushroom caps, stem sides down, on grill rack coated with cooking spray, and grill for 5 minutes on each side or until soft.

Spoon ¼ cup tomato mixture into each mushroom cap. Cover and grill 3 minutes or until cheese is melted. Sprinkle with parsley.

Jane VanFossen

Harvest Potatoes

32 OUNCES FROZEN HASH BROWN POTATOES, THAWED

1 CAN CREAM OF CHICKEN SOUP

8 OUNCES SOUR CREAM

8 OUNCES AMERICAN CHEESE, SHREDDED

½ CUP MARGARINE, MELTED

1 ½ TEASPOON SALT

1 MEDIUM ONION, DICED

TOPPING:

2 CUPS CORN FLAKES, CRUSHED

¼ CUP MARGARINE, MELTED

This recipe is a staple with many families. You will want to combine all ingredients in a greased 9x13 baking dish. Top with cornflake mixture. Bake at 350 degrees for 45 minutes.

Rameen Christensen

Macaroni and Cheese Casserole

1 ½ CUPS MACARONI
½ POUND CHEESE
1 ½ TEASPOONS PARSLEY
½ CUP BUTTER
1 ½ TABLESPOONS ONION
1 ½ TABLESPOONS PIMENTO
1 TEASPOON SALT
½ TEASPOON PEPPER
½ TEASPOONS PAPRIKA
2 EGGS
2 CUPS MILK

Cook macaroni 15 minutes. Drain. Put in buttered baking dish. Add butter, cubed cheese, onion, and seasonings. Beat eggs slightly and add hot milk. Pour over macaroni. Bake in an uncovered dish at 350 degrees for 50 minutes.

Alice Russell (Wade's great grandmother)

Mary's Peach Tea

TWO CUPS OF PEACH NECTAR
ONE CUP OF SUGAR
3 QUART SIZE TEA BAGS
TWO QUARTS OF WATER
ONE PINT OF ICE CUBES

Here is a short cut in preparation of this delicious peach tea. Pour two quarts of water into an automatic coffee pot. Place three quart size tea bags where you would place coffee, then brew. After tea has brewed remove from heat and pour one cup of sugar and one pint of ice cubes in mixture. Then add two cups of peach nectar and mix well.

If you choose to garnish, you may add a slice of lemon.

Mary Fallin

Homemade Strawberry Lemonade

1 CUP SUGAR

1 CUP OF WATER

1 PINT FRESH STRAWBERRIES

1 CUP FRESH LEMON JUICE
(THIS EQUALED CLOSE TO 8 OF MY LEMONS)

4-6 CUPS COLD WATER
(THIS WILL VARY DEPENDING ON YOUR TASTE)

To make a simple syrup you will combine the sugar with 1 cup of water in a saucepan. Then place over medium heat until the sugar is dissolved, stirring the pan with a spatula occasionally. Must let cool. After the simple syrup has cooled, puree strawberries in a blender with ½ cup water. Take a large pitcher, combine strawberry puree, simple syrup, and lemon juice. The amount of water you use will depend on your taste, so add a little at a time until perfection and personal balance is achieved. You may garnish with fresh strawberries served over ice.

Erica Miles

Left to right, standing: Vince VanFossen, First Gentleman Wade Christensen, Clay Christensen, and Drew Christensen. Seated: Jane VanFossen, Governor Mary Fallin, Gail Christensen, and Rameen Christensen.

Fruit Punch

4 ½ CUPS SUGAR

6 CUPS WATER

BRING TO A BOIL FOR 5 MINUTES AND COOL

MASH 5 BANANAS IN BLENDER

1 SMALL CAN FROZEN LEMONADE

1 SMALL CAN FROZEN ORANGE JUICE

2 QUARTS GINGER ALE

MIX AS DIRECTED

1 LARGE CAN PINEAPPLE JUICE

You will mix and blend the above mentioned ingredients and freeze. Set out 4-5 hours before serving. Add 2 quarts ginger ale. Serves 50.

Arlene Grimsley

GETTING GRILLED BY WADE CHRISTENSEN

Brittiany's Chocolate Sheet Cake

2 STICKS BUTTER
½ CUP WATER
4 TABLESPOONS COCOA
2 CUPS FLOUR, SIFTED
2 CUPS SUGAR
2 EGGS, BEATEN
1 TEASPOON SODA
1 CUP BUTTERMILK
¼ TEASPOON SALT

This recipe has to be Oklahoma's most favorite sheet cake. This is Brittiany's favorite request when Wade is baking. Heat together butter, water, and cocoa stirring constantly until butter is melted. Pour over flour and sugar. Add eggs, soda, buttermilk, and salt. Bake in greased jelly roll pan at 350 degrees for 25 minutes. Frost while warm. Cool about 5 minutes.

FROSTING:

1 STICK BUTTER
4 TABLESPOONS COCOA
6 TABLESPOONS MILK
1 POUND PACKAGE POWDERED SUGAR
1 TEASPOON VANILLA
1 CUP PECANS, CHOPPED

Melt butter, cocoa, and milk, stirring constantly. Pour this mixture over powdered sugar, vanilla, and nuts. Mix well and frost warm cake.

Brittiany Christensen

Coconut Pie

PIE CRUST:
1 CUP SELF-RISING FLOUR
½ CUP CRISCO
¼ CUP ICE WATER

Mix flour and Crisco with fork, add the ice water and mix until you can make a ball (add a little flour to keep from being sticky). Put flour on surface you are rolling it out on and on rolling pin. Roll out a little larger than pie pan, fold in half and put in pan, unfold and press into place. With your two fore-fingers crimp the sides of the crust, trim off excess dough, and take a fork to put air holes in crust. Bake at 350 degrees until done. Cool before filling.

FILLING:
3 CUPS MILK
1 CUP SUGAR
3 EGG YOLKS (USE WHITES FOR MERINGUE)
3 TABLESPOONS FLOUR
3 TABLESPOONS CORN STARCH
1 CUP COCONUT
1 TEASPOON VANILLA
2 TABLESPOONS BUTTER

Warm milk in sauce pan, add beaten yolks. In a separate bowl, mix sugar, flour, and corn starch, add to mixture and cook until starts to thicken (about 5 minutes). Add coconut and vanilla and cook until thick. Remove from heat and add butter, stirring until butter melts, and cook about ten minutes. Pour into crust.

Meringue:

Use the egg whites you separated and set aside while making the filling. Make sure you leave them at room temperature. Beat until light and fluffy, add ¼ cup sugar and 1 teaspoon vanilla. Mix well. Spoon onto top of filling. Sprinkle coconut on top of meringue. Bake until meringue is brown.

Mary Lee Gentry (Gail Christensen's Mother)

Oatmeal Cookies

1 ¼ CUPS SUGAR
1 CUP SHORTENING
2 EGGS
3 CUPS OATMEAL
½ CUP SOUR MILK
2 CUPS FLOUR
1 TEASPOON SODA
1 CUP RAISINS
1 TEASPOON CINNAMON
½ TEASPOON NUTMEG
½ TEASPOON GINGER
½ TEASPOON CLOVES

Mix all ingredients together and bake at 350 degrees.

Jo Christensen

Oklahoma Millionaires

1 CUP SUGAR
1 CUP BROWN SUGAR
1 CUP WHITE CORN SYRUP
½ POUND MARGARINE
1 CAN (14 OUNCE) EVAPORATED MILK
1 TEASPOON VANILLA
4 CUPS PECANS
DIPPING CHOCOLATE

Mix sugars, syrup, margarine, and 1 cup milk; bring to rolling boil. Keep mixture boiling slowly and add remaining milk. Cook to soft ball stage (234 degrees). Add vanilla and pecans. Pour into 9×9-inch pan. Refrigerate several hours. Cut into squares. Melt dipping chocolate and dip squares in mixture and put on waxed paper. Cool until firm.

Arlene Grimsley

German Chocolate Brownie

1 PACKAGE CARAMELS

1 PACKAGE GERMAN CHOCOLATE CAKE MIX

⅓ CUP EVAPORATED MILK

1 CUP CHOCOLATE CHIPS

½ CUP EVAPORATED MILK

¾ CUP MELTED MARGARINE

1 CUP PECANS

You must combine caramels and ½ cup evaporated milk in double boiler. Cook over low heat and stir until caramels melt. Set aside. In large bowl combine cake mix, margarine, and ⅓ cup evaporated milk and pecans. Press ½ the dough into a greased 9×13-inch pan. Bake at 350 degrees for 8 minutes. Spread caramel over baked crust. Sprinkle chocolate chips over the caramel. Crumble the other ½ of dough over chocolate chips layer. Return to oven and bake for 20 minutes.

Clay Christensen

Fresh Strawberry Pie

1 CUP PLUS 2 TABLESPOONS SUGAR

1 CUP WATER

⅛ TEASPOON SALT

3 TABLESPOONS CORNSTARCH

3 TABLESPOONS COLD WATER

3 HEAPING TABLESPOONS STRAWBERRY JELL-O

1 PINT FRESH STRAWBERRIES, SLICED

Mix and boil sugar, water, and salt. Blend cornstarch and cold water and stir into boiled mixture. Cook until clear. Add Jell-O. Cook, but do not jell. Add sliced strawberries. Pour into baked pie shell. Refrigerate and serve with Cool Whip. Optional: cover baked pie shell with sliced bananas, then add strawberry mixture.

BEEF, POULTRY, PORK & SEAFOOD

BBQ Smokey Strip Steaks

4 ¾ POUNDS NEW YORK STRIP STEAKS, CUT ½ INCH THICK
2 TABLESPOONS BBQ SEASONING (PERSONAL PREFERENCE)
3 DROPS HICKORY SMOKE
SALT AND COARSE GROUND PEPPER TO TASTE

You will want to cook on high heat. Rinse and pat dry steaks. Rub barbeque seasoning into steaks along with salt, pepper, and smoke. Grill over direct high heat until the internal temperature reaches 145 degrees for medium rare, about 8-10 minutes, turning once halfway through grilling time. Cook until desired to your taste.

Drew Christensen

Flank Steak with Lime Marinade

3 TABLESPOONS EXTRA VIRGIN OLIVE OIL

3 TABLESPOONS FRESH LIME JUICE (2)

3 TABLESPOONS FRESH LEMON JUICE

4 GARLIC CLOVES, THIN SLICED

1 SERRANO PEPPER, CORED, SEEDED IF DESIRED AND THINLY SLICED (OPTIONAL)

KOSHER SALT TO TASTE

1 ½ POUNDS FLANK STEAKS

You want to place your oil, lime and lemon juice, garlic, Serrano pepper, and salt in a shallow dish, stirring until well blended. Lay the flank steak in the dish and turn a few times until thoroughly coated. Cover with plastic wrap and place in refrigerator for 2 hours or overnight. Lightly oil the grill grate and prepare to medium-high grill. Pat the steak dry. Grill for 5 to 10 minutes, turning once. Let stand. Cut on slant across the grain.

Clay Christensen

The All-American Hamburger

2 TABLESPOONS CHOPPED ONION
2 TEASPOONS WORCESTERSHIRE SAUCE
2 TEASPOON S PREPARED MUSTARD
1 POUND GROUND BEEF OR GROUND CHUCK
4 SLICES AMERICAN CHEESE HALVED DIAGONALLY
2 SLICES SWISS CHEESE, HALVED DIAGONALLY
4 HAMBURGER BUNS, SPLIT AND TOASTED
LETTUCE LEAVES, ONIONS, SLICED TOMATOES, COOKED BACON PICKLES, KETCHUP, MUSTARD, AND MAYO

We combine the first three ingredients, combine with our meat. Then shape into four patties. Grill, covered over medium heat 6 minutes on each side or until temp is 160 degrees and juices run clear. Top each patty with 2 triangles of American and Swiss cheese. Serve hamburger with other toppings as desired.

Christensen Brothers—Wade, Drew & Clay

Black and Blue Burgers

1 POUND GROUND CHUCK
2 CLOVES MINCED GARLIC
1 TABLESPOON DIJON MUSTARD
2 GREEN ONIONS, CHOPPED
½ CUP (2 OUNCES) CRUMBLED BLUE CHEESE
1 EGG
1 TEASPOON WATER
SALT AND FRESH GROUND PEPPER

After combining all the ingredients, you want to form patties (½ inch thick). Place in refrigerator to chill. Turn grill to high heat. With these burgers you want to oil your grates. salt and pepper to taste. Grill 5 minutes per side. To hold juices and cheese in burger do not press down on the burger when cooking. Serve with choice of vegetables and mayo.

Price Fallin

THE FIRST GENTLEMAN BURGER

2 LBS OF LEAN HAMBURGER MEAT

2 SWEET ONIONS

SALT & PEPPER TO TASTE

LETTUCE

TOMATOES

SLICED CHEESE OF YOUR CHOICE

DILL PICKLES

KETCHUP

MUSTARD

HAMBURGER BUNS

This Burger can be made with almost everything grown in Oklahoma, including the canola oil, beef, lettuce, tomatoes, buns, cheese, onions, and pickles.   It is simple, traditional, and absolutely delicious. Heat Oklahoma grown canola oil in a skillet to 310°F. Chop onions and cook them in the canola oil until slightly brown and caramelized. Mix the cooked onions, hamburger meat, salt, and pepper in a bowl and then form the mixture into four ½-pound hamburger patties. Cook patties on a charcoal or gas grill until meat reaches an internal temperature of 160°F. Toast the hamburger buns. Top the hamburgers with your favorite condiments. This simple burger has been enjoyed by four generations of Christensens on the farm.

Grilled Portobello Burgers with Pesto Mayo

1 TABLESPOON EXTRA VIRGIN OLIVE OIL

1 TEASPOON GARLIC PASTE
(OR ½ TEASPOON PRESSED FRESH GARLIC)

KOSHER SALT AND PEPPER TO TASTE

4 PORTOBELLO MUSHROOMS (4 INCH), STEMS REMOVED,
GILLS SCRAPED FROM BENEATH CAPS

1 ½ TABLESPOONS BASIL PESTO

1 ½ TABLESPOONS REDUCED-FAT OLIVE OIL MAYONNAISE

1 TABLESPOON FRESH LEMON JUICE

8 SLICES FRESH MOZZARELLA CHEESE (¼ INCH THICK)

4 SANDWICH-SIZE ENGLISH MUFFINS, SPLIT, TOASTED

4 BUTTER-LEAF LETTUCE LEAVES

2 JARRED ROASTED BELL PEPPERS, QUARTERED

You want to cook these burgers on medium heat. Combining your oil, garlic paste, kosher salt, and freshly ground pepper to taste; lightly brush mixture over mushrooms. Stir pesto, mayonnaise, and lemon juice in a small bowl until smooth. Place mushroom caps on hot grill. Cook around 3 minutes per side, until tender, placing 2 slices cheese on top of each mushroom during your last minute of grilling. Next on one side of muffin spread pesto mayo. Then place lettuce leaves on the other side of muffin. Place your mushroom over lettuce and top with roasted peppers.

Christina Fallin

Grilled Chicken with **Peach Salsa**

- ½ **CUP CHOPPED ONION**
- 1 (14 ½ OUNCE) CAN WHOLE TOMATOES, DRAINED AND CHOPPED
- ⅔ **CUP DICED PEACHES**
- ½ **CUP PEACH PRESERVES**
- 1 **CINNAMON STICK**
- 1 **TABLESPOON CHOPPED FRESH CILANTRO**
- 1 TEASPOON CHOPPED FRESH GINGER ROOT OR ¼ TEASPOON DRIED GINGER
- ¼ **TEASPOON SALT**
- ⅛ **TEASPOON PEPPER**
- 3 WHOLE CHICKEN BREASTS, SKINNED, BONED, AND HALVED
- 3 **CUPS COOKED RICE**

You will want to spray a non-stick sauce pan with cooking spray so your sugar ingredients will not stick. You are going to cook this mixture over medium heat until hot. Add your onion and cook 3 minutes. Then add remaining ingredients and bring to a boil. Reduce heat, simmer uncovered 20-30 minutes or until sauce thickens. When ready to serve remove and discard cinnamon stick. Charcoal your chicken on a grill for approximately 20 minutes until tender. I would suggest you serve your chicken breast on top of rice, then pour salsa over chicken.

Mary Fallin

Grilled Pork Tenderloin with Fresh Peach and Ginger Sauce

1 TABLESPOON VEGETABLE OIL

1 CUP CHOPPED ONION

5 TABLESPOONS SUGAR

1 ½ CUPS DRY RED WINE

¾ CUP REDUCED-SODIUM SOY SAUCE

¼ CUP BALSAMIC VINEGAR

2 ½ TABLESPOONS FINELY CHOPPED PEELED FRESH GINGER

1 ½ TEASPOONS GROUND CINNAMON

½ TEASPOON COARSELY GROUND BLACK PEPPER

3 (14 TO 16 OUNCE) PORK TENDERLOINS

3 MEDIUM PEACHES, BLANCHED IN BOILING WATER 1 MINUTE, PEELED, PITTED, CHOPPED

2 TABLESPOONS CHOPPED FRESH CHIVES

In a heavy medium sauce pan heat oil over medium-high heat. Next you will add onion and sugar. Saute chopped onions for 6 minutes. Pour in wine and next five ingredients stirring 1 minute longer. Remove from heat and cool sauce completely. Place pork in a resealable large plastic bag. Pour 1 cup of sauce in bag with pork. Seal and refrigerate at least 6 hours. Take your remaining sauce and refrigerate separately. Remove pork from marinade and place on grill, turning occasionally and cook roughly 35 minutes. Next you will boil remaining sauce in heavy saucepan reducing liquid by half, about 5 minutes. Add peaches. Place your pork on platter with sauce poured over top and sprinkle with chives.

Rameen Christensen

Grilled Pork Medallions
with Melon Salsa

1 WHOLE PORK TENDERLOIN
   (1 ¼ POUNDS), TRIMMED OF FAT
5 LIMES
1 TABLESPOON OLIVE OIL
½ CUP LOOSELY PACKED FRESH
   CILANTRO LEAVES, CHOPPED
SALT AND PEPPER
2 CUPS CHOPPED CANTALOUPE
1 CUP CHOPPED HONEYDEW
1 CUP WATERMELON
1 JALAPENO, MINCED

You will cut tenderloin crosswise into 8 equal pieces. Firmly press with palm of hand on cut side of each piece to flatten to about 1-inch-thick medallion. From remaining limes, grate 1 teaspoon; peel and squeeze ¼ cup juice. In small bowl, combine oil, ½ teaspoon lime peel, half of the cilantro, ⅛ teaspoon salt, and ⅛ teaspoon coarsely ground black pepper. Rub cilantro mixture on pork medallions to season both sides. Place pork on hot grill and cook 4 minutes. Turn pork over. Add lime halves, cut sides down, to same grill and cook 3 to 4 minutes, or until lightly browned and warm. Cook pork 4 to 5 minutes longer, or until browned on outside and still slightly pink in center. Meanwhile, in medium bowl, combine melons, jalapeno, lime juice, ⅛ teaspoon salt, and remaining cilantro and lime peel. Makes about 3 cups salsa. Serve pork with melon salsa and grilled limes to squeeze over pork.

Gail Christensen

Grilled Baby Back Ribs

RUB
1 TEASPOON ONION POWDER
1 TEASPOON GARLIC POWDER
SALT AND PEPPER TO TASTE
5 DROPS OF LIQUID SMOKE
COMBINE ALL INGREDIENTS IN A BOWL

2 (1 ½ POUNDS) RACKS OF BABY BACK RIBS
LIQUID SMOKE, HICKORY, OR MESQUITE
SALT AND PEPPER TO TASTE
1 TEASPOON GARLIC POWDER TO TASTE

Rinse and pat dry ribs. Rub a few drops of liquid smoke into meat. Rub salt and pepper and garlic powder into meat. Then coat generously with barbeque sauce. Let stand in refrigerator for 3 hours. Place racks on grill. Cook until desired taste and tenderness.

Blake Christensen

Grilled BBQ Bacon Shrimp

16 (10 INCH) WOODEN SKEWERS
2 TABLESPOONS BUTTER
½ CUP FINELY CHOPPED ONIONS
1 SMALL JALAPENO, SEEDED AND CHOPPED
½ TEASPOON CAYENNE PEPPER
SALT AND FRESHLY GROUND BLACK PEPPER
1 (1 INCH) PIECE OF GINGER, GRATED
½ CUP DARK BROWN SUGAR
¼ CUP ORANGE JUICE
1 CUP KETCHUP
16 COLOSSAL SHRIMP, SHELLED
    WITH TAIL ON, DEVEINED (1 ¼ POUNDS)
4 SLICES BACON

Preheat grill to medium. Soak skewers in water while preparing sauce. In a medium saucepan melt butter and sauté onions and jalapeno until tender. Season with cayenne, salt, and pepper. Add ginger, brown sugar, orange juice, and ketchup in that order making sure to blend each ingredient completely before adding the next. Let simmer until edges begin to caramelize, about 15 minutes. Set aside. Once cool remove half of the sauce and reserve for dining. The other half is for brushing on the shrimp when grilling. Cut bacon in thirds. Thread each shrimp onto a skewer, starting from the tail end. Bend the shrimp as you thread it so it lies in 1 straight line on the skewer, removing the natural curve. Wrap the center of each shrimp with a piece of bacon. Brush with BBQ sauce and place skewers with bacon seam side down onto the grill. Cook over medium heat until bacon crisps and shrimp is cooked through, about 8 minutes.

Trey Christensen

BBQ Shrimp & Peach Kabobs

12 METAL OR BAMBOO SKEWERS (12 INCH)

1 TABLESPOON PACKED DARK BROWN SUGAR

1 TEASPOON SWEET PAPRIKA

¼ TEASPOON CAYENNE (GROUND RED PEPPER)

SALT AND PEPPER TO TASTE

1 POUND SHRIMP (16 TO 20 COUNT),
SHELLED AND DEVEINED

3 MEDIUM PEACHES, CUT INTO 1-INCH CHUNKS

**1 BUNCH GREEN ONIONS, DARK GREEN PARTS
TRIMMED, CUT INTO 2-INCH PIECES**

LIME WEDGES, FOR SERVING

Soak your bamboo skewers in cold water at least 30 minutes to prevent burning. Direct grilling on high. Combine brown sugar, paprika, cayenne, and salt and pepper to taste in a large bowl. Add peaches, onions, and shrimp; toss until fully coated. Thread shrimp, peaches, and onion alternately onto skewers. You will want to cook on high 3 or 4 minutes, turning once. Try lime wedges when serving.

Trent Christensen

GETTING GRILLED BY WADE CHRISTENSEN

Tequila-Lime Shrimp

2 ½ POUNDS UNPEELED, LARGE FRESH SHRIMP

½ CUP OLIVE OIL

1 CUP FRESH LIME JUICE

¼ CUP TEQUILA

2 SHALLOTS, CHOPPED

2 GARLIC CLOVES, MINCED

SALT AND PEPPER TO TASTE

1 TEASPOON GROUND CUMIN

First you will peel shrimp, leaving tails intact; devein. Next you will combine oil and remaining ingredients in large bowl; stir in shrimp. Cover and chill 1 hour. Remove shrimp from marinade, start threading 9 shrimp per skewer. Coat food rack with cooking spray and place shrimp on medium-high heat 3 to 4 minutes on each side.

Clay Christensen

Grilled Fresh Tuna

4 (4 TO 5 OUNCE) TUNA STEAKS (¾ INCH THICK)
½ CUP ORANGE JUICE
½ CUP SOY SAUCE
2 TABLESPOONS KETCHUP
2 TABLESPOONS CHOPPED FRESH PARSLEY
3 TABLESPOONS LEMON JUICE
1 GARLIC CLOVE, MINCED
⅛ TEASPOON GROUND WHITE PEPPER

Let's start by placing tuna in a large heavy zip-top plastic bag. Combine orange juice and remaining ingredients and pour over tuna. You will need to refrigerate in sealed bag for 1 hour. Remove tuna and reserve marinade. Place remaining marinade in small saucepan, bringing to a boil. Next you will coat food rack with cooking spray. Place tuna steaks on rack, grilling with covered lid, 3 to 4 minutes on each side.

Blake Christensen

Grilled Catfish with Fresh Tomato Relish

4 (6-OUNCE) CATFISH FILETS*
1 TABLESPOON OLIVE OIL
SALT AND PEPPER TO TASTE
FRESH TOMATO RELISH (RECIPE FOLLOWS)

You will spray grill rack and heat grill to medium-high. Brush catfish with oil and sprinkle with salt and pepper. Grill with covered lid, 3 to 4 minutes per side. My suggestion is to use U.S. Farm-Raised Catfish*. Serve with tomato relish spread on top of fish. This dish is rich in color.

Fresh Tomato Relish
Makes about 2 cups

3 CUPS SEEDED AND DICED TOMATOES
3 TABLESPOONS MINCED GREEN ONION
1 TABLESPOON MINCED FRESH CILANTRO
2 TABLESPOONS FRESH LIME JUICE
SALT AND PEPPER TO TASTE

Place ingredients in a small bowl. Cover and chill for up to 3 days.

Kayli Boelte

Citrus-Basil Salmon

3 TABLESPOONS BASIL OLIVE OIL

4 TABLESPOONS FRESH LEMON JUICE

4 TABLESPOONS FRESH LIME JUICE

1 ½ TEASPOONS GRATED LEMON ZEST

1 ½ TEASPOONS GRATED LIME ZEST

SALT AND PEPPER TO TASTE

4 SKINLESS SALMON FILETS, ABOUT
   1 TO 1 ¼ INCH THICK (7 TO 8 OUNCES EACH)

STRIPS OF FRESH BASIL LEAVES, LEMON
   ZEST, AND LIME ZEST (FOR GARNISH)

Whisk together in a large shallow bowl 3 tablespoons basil oil, 3 tablespoons lemon juice, 3 tablespoons lime juice, ½ teaspoon lemon zest, ½ teaspoon grated lime zest, salt and pepper to taste. Next we will add over salmon, coating filets generously. Place salmon filets directly on medium-high grill. Cook 5-6 minutes turning once. Cover filets with remaining ingredients.

Mary Fallin

Grilled Lobster Tails

4 FROZEN 5-6 OZ. ROCK LOBSTER TAILS
¾ TO 1 CUP BUTTER, MELTED
1 TABLESPOON LEMON JUICE
PINCH OF GARLIC POWDER

Thaw lobster tails first, cutting off the thin undershell membrane with scissors or sharp knife. Insert long skewers lengthwise between the shell and meat to prevent curling. Combine butter, lemon juice, and garlic powder in small bowl. Brush this mixture over lobster meat. With meat side up, grill lobster tails over high heat for 6-7 minutes. Brush with sauce and turn shell side up, grilling 6-8 minutes or until meat is opaque (light) and has no transparency. Serve immediately with or without remaining sauce.

Alex Christensen
Wade Christensen

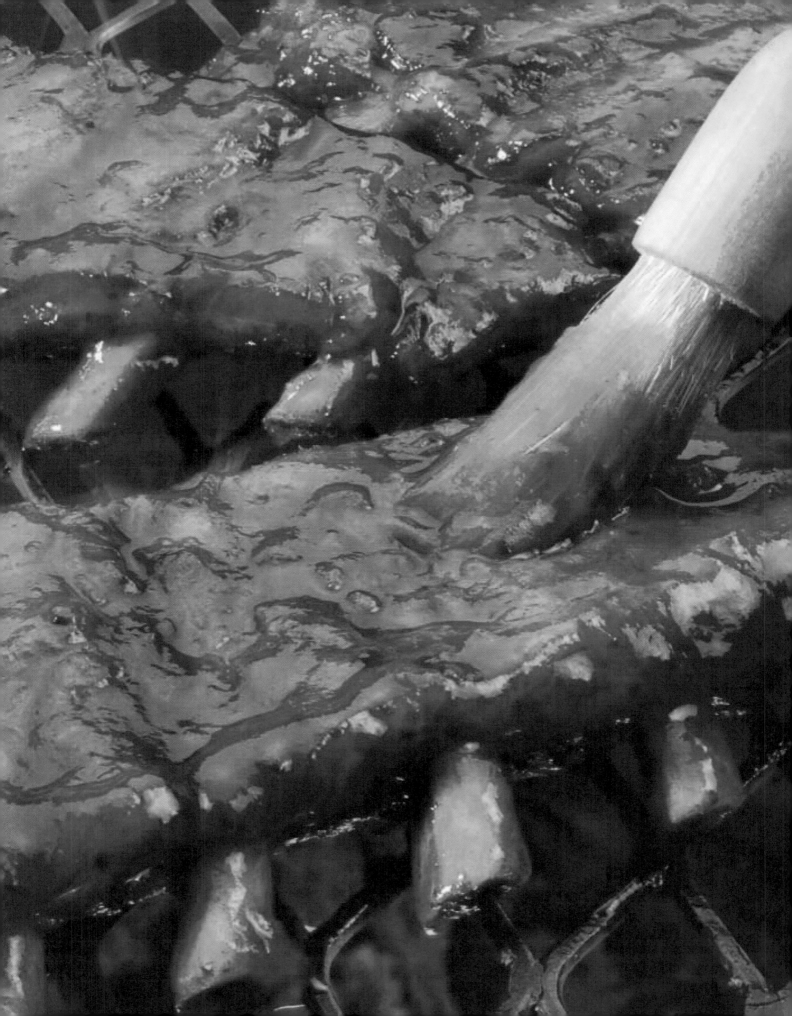

RUBS, MARINADES, SAUCES & SALSAS

The history of grilling rubs can be traced back thousands of years to as early as 5000 B.C. The rubs have not only been used to flavor meats and vegetables, but for medicinal uses as well. By using rubs, you can cause your food to have a better flavor and be healthier for you as well.

Some even refer to rubs as spice rubs, in which spices are rubbed into vegetables and meat. Most of the spices used are course ground for maximum flavoring and tenderizing of the food. Rubs can have anything from pepper to sugar and salt and garlic in their mixes.

Argentinean Marinade

1 BUNCH PARSLEY, CHOPPED
8 GARLIC CLOVES
¾ CUP OLIVE OIL
¼ CUP LEMON JUICE, FRESHLY SQUEEZED
2 TEASPOONS CAYENNE
¾ CUP ONION, YELLOW/SMALL DICE
1 BUNCH CILANTRO, CHOPPED
1 ROASTED BELL PEPPER
1 TABLESPOON OREGANO, FRESH
1 TABLESPOON PAPRIKA, SMOKED
1 TEASPOON CUMIN
SALT AND PEPPER TO TASTE

Combine all ingredients in a blender or food processor and pulse until mixed well. Marinate meat up to 24 hours.

Chef Robin L. Obert

Asian Marinade

Combine all ingredients. Marinate between 4-6 hours.

Chef Robin L. Obert

⅔ CUP TERIYAKI
2 TABLESPOONS GINGER, FRESH
2 TEASPOONS LEMONGRASS PASTE
¼ CUP TOASTED SESAME OIL
SYRACHA TO TASTE
1 TABLESPOON TOASTED SESAME SEEDS
¼ CUP PINEAPPLE JUICE
2 TABLESPOONS HONEY
2 TABLESPOONS RICE WINE VINEGAR
1 TABLESPOON LIME ZEST
1 TABLESPOON GARLIC PASTE
2 TABLESPOONS SHALLOT, OR GREEN ONION

Balsamic Marinade

1 CUP BALSAMIC VINEGAR

3 TABLESPOONS GARLIC CLOVE, MINCED

½ CUP OLIVE OIL

1 ROSEMARY SPRIG

3 OREGANO SPRIGS, FRESH

1 TEASPOON CRUSHED RED PEPPER, OR TO TASTE

Combine all ingredients. Marinate pork or chicken up to six hours.

Chef Robin L. Obert

Tropical Marinade

¾ CUP PINEAPPLE JUICE

4 TABLESPOONS APRICOT PRESERVES

1 TEASPOON GROUND GINGER

1 TEASPOON DRY MUSTARD

½ TEASPOON SALT

In a small bowl, whisk together pineapple juice, preserves, ginger, dry mustard, and salt until well blended. Pour mixture over chicken and refrigerate to marinate meat for 3 to 4 hours, turning occasionally.

Price Fallin

Rich Beef Rub

¼ CUP SALT

3 TABLESPOONS PAPRIKA

2 TABLESPOONS COARSE BLACK PEPPER

2 TEASPOONS ONION POWDER

2 TEASPOONS GARLIC POWDER

1 ½ TEASPOONS CAYENNE PEPPER

½ TEASPOON CORIANDER

½ TEASPOON TURMERIC

Combine salt, paprika, black pepper, onion powder, garlic powder, cayenne pepper, coriander, and turmeric in a small bowl, mixing well. You must store in an airtight container. This rub will yield ½ cup.

Wade, Clay & Drew Christensen

All-Purpose Chicken Rub

3 ½ TABLESPOONS OF PAPRIKA

2 TABLESPOONS BLACK PEPPER

1 ½ TABLESPOONS CELERY SALT

2 TABLESPOONS SUGAR

1 TEASPOON ONION POWDER

1 ½ TEASPOONS DRY MUSTARD

½ TEASPOON CAYENNE PEPPER

2 TEASPOONS FINELY GRATED LEMON PEEL

Combine paprika, black pepper, celery salt, sugar, onion powder, dry mustard, cayenne pepper, and lemon, put in small container. Refrigerate in an airtight container.

Wade, Clay & Drew Christensen

All-Purpose Pork Rub

1 ½ TABLESPOONS PAPRIKA
2 TEASPOONS SALT
2 TEASPOONS SUGAR
2 TEASPOONS BROWN SUGAR
2 TEASPOONS GROUND CUMIN
1 ½ TEASPOONS CAYENNE PEPPER
2 TEASPOONS BLACK PEPPER

Combine paprika, salt, sugar, brown sugar, cumin, cayenne pepper, and black pepper in small container. You may use this rub with many cuts of pork.

Wade, Clay & Drew Christensen

Chipotle Ketchup

1 ½ CUPS REGULAR KETCHUP
2 TABLESPOONS PUREED CANNED CHIPOTLE IN ADOBO SAUCE
SALT AND PEPPER TO TASTE

Whisk all of the above ingredients in a small bowl. Cover and refrigerate for 45 minutes to an hour. This ketchup can be refrigerated in an airtight container for at least 2 weeks.

Wade, Clay & Drew Christensen

Gorgonzola Butter

3 TABLESPOONS CRUMBLED GORGONZOLA CHEESE

3 TABLESPOONS CREAM CHEESE SPREAD WITH CHIVES AND ONIONS

3 TABLESPOONS BUTTER SOFTENED

1 TABLESPOON CHOPPED PINE NUTS OR WALNUTS, TOASTED

Combine Gorgonzola cheese, cream cheese, butter, and nuts in a small bowl and mix. Shape your mixture into 1-inch-diameter log. Wrap in plastic and chill approximately 1 hour. Place 2 slices of butter per New York Strip Steak or your favorite cut of meat.

Wade Christensen

Peach and Wild Blackberry Salsa

3 LARGE PEACHES (FIRM AND RIPE, PEELED, STONE REMOVED AND DICED INTO ½" PIECES)

4 CUPS FRESH BLACKBERRIES

½ LARGE SWEET RED PEPPER, SEEDED AND DICED SMALL

½ LARGE RED ONION, CHOPPED SMALL

1 MEDIUM JALAPENO PEPPER, SEEDED AND CHOPPED VERY SMALL

8 TABLESPOONS FRESHLY SQUEEZED LIME JUICE (ABOUT 3 TO 4 LARGE LIMES)

¼ CUP FRESHLY SQUEEZED ORANGE JUICE

¼ CUP LIQUID HONEY

Place and prepare peaches in large bowl. You will wash and pat dry blackberries. Add sweet red pepper, red onion, jalapeno peppers, lime juice, orange juice, and honey, blending well. Fold in blackberries, trying not to mash them. Chill and serve with grilled fish.

Salsa Fresca

1 POUND RIPE TOMATOES
   (3 TO 4 MEDIUM) CHOPPED

⅓ CUP CHOPPED SWEET ONION
   (PURPLE OR VIDALIA)

¼ CUP FRESH, CHOPPED
   CILANTRO LEAVES

3 TABLESPOONS LIME JUICE

1 JALAPENO, SEEDED AND MINCED

SALT AND PEPPER TO TASTE

Gently blend all ingredients in medium bowl. Next you will cover and refrigerate for 1 to 8 hours. I suggest you drain before serving.

Mary Fallin

Black Bean Salsa

1 BUNCH GREEN ONIONS, CHOPPED

2 CANS BLACK BEANS, DRAINED
   AND RINSED

1 LARGE PACKAGE FROZEN CORN

4 TOMATOES, DICED

½ BUNCH CILANTRO, CHOPPED

¼ TEASPOON CUMIN

SALT AND PEPPER TO TASTE

JUICE OF 2 LIMES

1 TABLESPOON CHOPPED JALAPENO

In a medium bowl combine all ingredients and chill before serving.

Adam Christensen

SUPERB SALADS, APPETIZERS, BREADS & SOUPS

Watermelon Fruit Salad

½ CUP SUGAR

¼ CUP WATER

5 CUPS CUBED SEEDLESS WATERMELON

2 CUPS SLICED STRAWBERRIES

1 CUP CUBED PINEAPPLE TIDBITS

1 CUP DICED KIWI

1 CUP CUBED MANGO

1 CUP FRESH RASPBERRIES

1 LIME, JUICED

GARNISH: MINT

Combine sugar and water in a large bowl. Next you will add watermelon, strawberries, pineapple, kiwi, mango, raspberries, and lime juice. Mix gently. Refrigerate 30 minutes or more before serving.

Staci Butler

Watermelon and Feta Salad

2 TABLESPOONS OLIVE OIL

2 TABLESPOONS WHITE WINE VINEGAR

2 TABLESPOONS FRESH LIME JUICE

SALT AND PEPPER TO TASTE

¼ SMALL RED ONION, THINLY SLICED

3 CUPS SEEDLESS WATERMELON, RIND REMOVED, CUT INTO THIN CHUNKS

2 CUPS SEEDLESS CUCUMBERS, CUT IN HALF HORIZONTALLY AND SLICED

3 CUPS BABY FIELD GREENS

3 OUNCES FETA CHEESE, CRUMBLED

Whisk together oil, vinegar, lime juice, salt, and pepper in bowl. Add onion, watermelon, cucumber, and baby field greens. Toss gently to combine. Sprinkle salad with feta cheese.

Chef Robin L. Obert

Chopped Tomato and **Cucumber Salad** with **Feta Cheese**

IN A MEDIUM BOWL:

1 HEAD CHOPPED LETTUCE (ICEBERG)

2 PINTS RIPE GRAPE OR CHERRY TOMATOES, HALVED LENGTHWISE OR SLICED

¼ CUP LIGHTLY CHOPPED MINT (OPTIONAL)

1 TABLESPOON CHOPPED FRESH THYME (OPTIONAL)

KOSHER SALT AND FRESHLY GROUND BLACK PEPPER TO TASTE

½ POUND FETA COARSELY CRUMBLED (2 CUPS)

1 LEMON ZEST FINELY GRATED

1 TABLESPOON + JUICED (¼ CUP) LEMON

2 ENGLISH CUCUMBERS, CUT INTO ½" DICE (4 CUPS)

4 SCALLIONS (WHITE AND GREEN PARTS)

1 SMALL CHOPPED, PURPLE ONION – TRIMMED AND THINLY SLICED (1/2 CUP)

2 ½ CUPS PITTED BLACK OLIVES

⅓ CUP EXTRA-VIRGIN OLIVE OIL

½ TABLESPOON SUGAR

Chop all ingredients and combine. Add feta cheese.

Gail Christensen

GETTING GRILLED BY WADE CHRISTENSEN

Southwestern Corn and Black Bean Salad

9 EARS FRESH CORN, SHUCKED

2 RED BELL PEPPERS, HALVED AND SEEDED

1 POBLANO PEPPER, HALVED AND SEEDED

5 TABLESPOONS LIME JUICE

3 TABLESPOONS OLIVE OIL

SALT TO TASTE

2 (15.5-OUNCE) CANS SEASONED BLACK BEANS, DRAINED AND RINSED

4 TABLESPOONS CHOPPED, FRESH CILANTRO

Grill corn for 5 minutes per side until tender on medium-high heat. Then grill bell peppers and poblano pepper for 3-4 minutes per side until blackened. Set aside while cutting kernels from corn cobs and chop peppers. Whisk together lime juice, olive oil, and salt in large bowl. Next stir in corn kernels, chopped peppers, beans, and cilantro, tossing well with dressing. Cover and chill before serving. This recipe takes a little extra effort, but the taste is worth the time.

Barb Morrow

Grape Salad

2 CUPS SEEDLESS GRAPES
(GREEN, RED, OR BOTH)

2 CUPS FINELY CHOPPED BROCCOLI

1 CUP RAISINS

1 POUND BACON, FRIED AND CRUMBLED

3 OUNCES SUNFLOWER SEEDS

1 TABLESPOON FINELY CHOPPED ONION

DRESSING:

1 CUP MAYONNAISE

¼ CUP MILK

¼ CUP SUGAR

2 TABLESPOONS LEMON JUICE

Mix seedless grapes, finely chopped broccoli, raisins, crumbled bacon, sunflower seeds, and finely chopped onion, toss gently. In separate bowl, whisk mayonnaise, milk, sugar, lemon juice, then pour over salad and toss well. This recipe is best when refrigerated over night.

Ronnye Perry Sharp

Strawberry Pretzel Salad

Mix crushed pretzels, melted butter, and 4 tablespoons of sugar then press mixture into bottom of a 9×13 inch baking dish. Bake at 400 degrees for 8 to 10 minutes until set. Set aside to cool. Then in a large bowl cream together cream cheese and 1 cup of sugar. Fold in whipped topping and spread mixture onto crust. Dissolve gelatin in boiling water, stirring in frozen strawberries and allow to set. When mixture is about the consistency of egg whites, pour and spread over cream cheese layer. Refrigerate for at least 1 hour.

2 ½ CUPS CRUSHED PRETZELS

1 CUP BUTTER, MELTED

4 TABLESPOONS WHITE SUGAR

1 (8 OUNCE) PACKAGE CREAM CHEESE, SOFTENED

1 CUP WHITE SUGAR

1 (8 OUNCE) CONTAINER FROZEN WHIPPED TOPPING, THAWED

2 (3 OUNCE) PACKAGES STRAWBERRY FLAVORED GELATIN

2 CUPS BOILING WATER

2 (10 OUNCE) PACKAGES FROZEN STRAWBERRIES

Kimmy Christensen

Strawberry/Spinach Salad

1 BAG OF BABY SPINACH

½-1 POUND OF SLICED MUSHROOMS

1 POUND OF SLICED STRAWBERRIES

⅓ TO ½ CUP OF CRUMBLED FETA CHEESE TO TASTE

1 2 OUNCE PACKAGE OF FRITO LAY PRALINE PECANS, CHOPPED

Mix all ingredients together. Use Maple Grove Farms of Vermont Fat Free Raspberry Vinaigrette to taste, tossing well.

Ronnye Perry Sharp

Governor Mary Fallin, First Gentleman Wade Christensen, and co-author Ronnye Perry Sharp in the kitchen of the Governor's Mansion.

Spinach Salad with Blackberries and Balsamic Vinaigrette

5 OUNCE CONTAINER, BABY SPINACH, WASHED
1 ½ PINTS FRESH BLACKBERRIES
½ PINT CHERRY TOMATOES, QUARTERED
2 GREEN ONIONS (SCALLIONS), SLICED
4 OUNCES FETA CHEESE, CRUMBLED
3 TABLESPOONS TOASTED PINE NUTS OR WALNUTS, CHOPPED
PINCH SALT AND PEPPER
BALSAMIC VINAIGRETTE

In a large container, combine spinach, blackberries, tomatoes, green onions, feta cheese, nuts, salt and pepper, and balsamic dressing to your taste. Toss and serve. Elegant and simple.

Gail Christensen

Avocado Citrus Salad

Whisk together cider vinegar, vegetable oil, sugar, and salt in separate bowl. Place greens in a large bowl, adding orange sections, grapefruit sections, pear slices, avocado slices, and grapes. Drizzle with dressing, tossing gently. Sprinkle walnuts on top.

Kayli Boelte

4 TABLESPOONS CIDER VINEGAR
2 TABLESPOONS VEGETABLE OIL
2 TABLESPOONS SUGAR
SALT TO TASTE
8 CUPS TORN SALAD GREENS
2 ORANGES, PEELED AND SECTIONED
1 LARGE GRAPEFRUIT, PEELED AND SECTIONED
1 PEAR, PEELED AND THINLY SLICED
3 RIPE AVOCADOS, PEELED AND SLICED
1 CUP SEEDLESS GREEN GRAPES
2 TABLESPOONS CHOPPED WALNUTS, TOASTED (OPTIONAL)

Macaroni Salad

In a large bowl, combine mayonnaise, sour cream, and mustard. Add celery, tomatoes, green onion, and macaroni. Stir to combine. Season with salt and pepper. Cover and refrigerate. Taste and adjust seasoning with salt and pepper. Serve cold.

Nola Christensen

½ CUP MAYONNAISE

½ CUP SOUR CREAM

2 TABLESPOONS WHOLE-GRAIN MUSTARD

3 RIBS CELERY, FINELY CHOPPED

3 LARGE TOMATOES, CORED AND DICED

4 GREEN ONIONS, WHITE AND GREEN PARTS, CHOPPED

1 POUND ELBOW MACARONI, COOKED

KOSHER SALT

GROUND BLACK PEPPER

Layered Shrimp and Avocado Salad

7 CUPS TORN ROMAINE LETTUCE

3 CUPS CHOPPED TOMATOES

4 DICED AVOCADOS

1 POUND OF COOKED SHRIMP

1 SLICED RED ONION

1 PACKAGE (10 OUNCES) THAWED FROZEN PEAS

1 ½ CUPS OF ITALIAN BOTTLED DRESSING

6 PIECES OF CRUMBLED BACON

In a trifle bowl, layer lettuce, tomatoes, avocados, shrimp, sliced red onion, and frozen peas. Pour Italian dressing evenly over top of salad. Sprinkle crumbed bacon over dressing.

Rameen Christensen

Flank Steak with Tomato, Cucumber and Watermelon Salad

2 TABLESPOONS EXTRA-VIRGIN OLIVE OIL

3 TABLESPOONS FRESH LIME JUICE

2 TEASPOONS LIME ZEST

½ CUP CILANTRO, CHOPPED

½ CUP SLICED SCALLIONS

SALT TO TASTE

1 ½ POUNDS FLANK STEAK

4 TOMATOES ON THE VINE, SEEDED AND DICED

2 CUCUMBERS, DICED

3 CUPS DICED WATERMELON

In medium container whisk oil, lime juice, zest, half the cilantro, half the scallions, and salt to make a dressing. Pour half into a large resealable plastic bag, adding steak. Place in refrigerator for 30 minutes or more. Toss tomatoes, cucumbers, and watermelon with remaining dressing, cilantro, scallions, and salt. Grill steak on medium-high 5 to 7 minutes on each side. Let steak rest for 10 minutes and slice steak against the grain. Serve steak with salad.

Wade and Mary

Cheese Spread with Strawberry Preserves

2 (16 OUNCE) PACKAGES SHARP CHEDDAR CHEESE*
2 (10 OUNCE) PACKAGES MILD CHEDDAR CHEESE*
1 MEDIUM WHITE ONION, FINELY CHOPPED
1 BUNCH GREEN ONIONS, FINELY CHOPPED
½ TEASPOON CAYENNE PEPPER
1 CUP MAYONNAISE
½ CUP CHOPPED PECANS, FINELY BUTTERED

Left to right, standing: Vince VanFossen, First Gentleman Wade Christensen, Clay Christensen, and Drew Christensen. Seated: Jane VanFossen, Governor Mary Fallin, Gail Christensen, and Rameen Christensen.

Grate the cheese and place in a large bowl. Finely chop the onions and add to the cheese. Add cayenne pepper and mayonnaise. Stir together or mix together with hands until it forms a ball. It may be necessary to add more mayonnaise to hold together. Butter a large mold and sprinkle with chopped pecans. Spread the pecans around the surface to coat the mold. Press in the cheese mixture and refrigerate overnight. To unmold, dip into hot water for a few seconds and turn upside down on a platter. Fill the center with strawberry preserves and serve with buttery crackers. Apricot preserves may be used in place of the strawberry preserves.

*It is important to grate the cheese instead of buying shredded cheese. Shredded cheese has a coating of corn starch on it to keep it from clumping together, therefore, it will not adhere in a ring or ball.

Wade and Mary

Ronnye's Cheeseball

2 (8 OUNCE) PACKAGES PHILADELPHIA CREAM CHEESE

1 BUNCH GREEN ONION TOPS, FINELY CHOPPED

1 (6 OUNCE) PACKAGE OSCAR MEYER SMOKED, SLICED HAM, CHOPPED VERY FINE

3 TABLESPOONS ACCENT

FINELY CHOPPED PECANS OR WALNUTS

Let cream cheese sit for two hours at room temperature, then blend together cream cheese, onions, ham, and accent. Shape and mold in the form of a ball. Roll in finely chopped nuts, covering entire cheese ball. Refrigerate before serving. You may decorate with holly berry leaves on top. Serve with Wheat Thins or Pecan Toasted Wheat Thins.

Ronnye Perry Sharp

Stuffed Cheese Mushrooms

24 FRESH MUSHROOMS, STEMS REMOVED

1 (10-OUNCE) PACKAGE FROZEN SPINACH, CHOPPED

2 OUNCES CREAM CHEESE

4 OUNCES FETA CHEESE

¼ CUP FINELY CHOPPED GREEN ONION

SALT AND PEPPER TO TASTE

1 CUP FRESH GRATED PARMESAN CHEESE

You may want to wipe mushrooms with a paper towel. Thaw spinach in a colander squeezing out excess moisture. Combine all ingredients except mushrooms and Parmesan in medium bowl, mixing well. Stuff mushroom caps with mixture and place on a cookie sheet. Sprinkle Parmesan cheese on top. Bake approximately 15-20 minutes. Serve warm.

Smoky Guacamole

4 AVOCADOS

1 ½ LIMES (JUICED)

1 RED ONION
(MEDIUM/SMALL DICED)

¼ TEASPOON CILANTRO

2 TABLESPOONS
CHIPOTLE IN ADOBO
(CHOPPED FINE)

1 TOMATO
(LARGE/SMALL DICED)

1 CLOVE GARLIC (MINCED)

1 JALAPENO
(MEDIUM/SMALL DICED)

2 TABLESPOONS
SOUR CREAM

1 TEASPOON SALT

1 TEASPOON PEPPER

Scoop out avocados in a medium bowl. Smash lightly with a fork. Stir in remaining ingredients and mix well. Place in serving bowl, lightly coat with lime juice, and place plastic wrap directly on top of guacamole until ready to serve. This will keep the guacamole from browning.

Chef Robin L. Obert

Robin L. Obert is chef at the Oklahoma Governor's Mansion.

Roasted Corn
and Avocado Dip

2 CUPS FRESH OR FROZEN WHOLE KERNEL CORN,
    THAWED AND PATTED DRY

2 TEASPOONS OLIVE OIL

3 RIPE AVOCADOS, PEELED AND CHOPPED

1 CUP SEEDED, DICED TOMATO

3 TABLESPOONS LIME JUICE

3 TABLESPOONS CHOPPED FRESH CILANTRO

2 TABLESPOONS MINCED ONION

2 SMALL CANNED JALAPENO PEPPERS, SEEDED
    AND DICED

1 GARLIC CLOVE, MINCED

SALT TO TASTE

Place corn and oil in a shallow pan and bake at 475 degrees for approximately 15 minutes. Cool corn and combine with chopped avocado and remaining ingredients, blending well. Cover and chill for 8 hours. We like to serve this dip with tortilla chips.

Vince and Jane VanFossen

Loaded Potato Skins

2 LARGE POTATOES (ABOUT 1 POUND),
    EACH CUT LENGTHWISE INTO 4 WEDGES
3 TABLESPOONS BUTTER, MELTED
2 TABLESPOONS PICANTE SAUCE
½ CUP SHREDDED CHEDDAR CHEESE
2 TABLESPOONS BACON BITS, DIVIDED
¼ CUP CHOPPED TOMATOES
2 TABLESPOONS CHOPPED GREEN ONION
3 TABLESPOONS MAYONNAISE
2 TABLESPOONS SOUR CREAM
1 TEASPOON RANCH DRESSING

Grill potatoes until done on medium-hot heat. Next remove pulp from potatoes, leaving a ¼ inch thick shell. Brush with butter. Evenly place picante sauce, cheese, and 1 tablespoon bacon bits among potato skins. Grill potatoes with lid open, skin side down, around 5 minutes. Then close lid and cook 2 minutes longer. Remove from grill and top with tomatoes and onion. In a small bowl, blend mayonnaise, sour cream, dressing, and remaining bacon bits. Serve with potatoes.

Bryant VanFossen

Poor-Man's Caviar

1 ½ TEASPOONS CUMIN SEEDS

2 (15 OUNCE) CANS BLACK BEANS, RINSED AND DRAINED

2 (15 ½ OUNCE) CAN WHOLE KERNEL CORN – DRAINED

1 RED PEPPER, MINCED

1 SMALL PURPLE ONION, MINCED (1 CUP)

¼ CUP CHOPPED FRESH CILANTRO

¼ CUP CHOPPED FRESH PARSLEY

1/3 CUP LIME JUICE

¼ CUP OLIVE OIL

2 CLOVES GARLIC, CRUSHED

1 TEASPOON DRIED CRUSHED RED PEPPER

SALT AND PEPPER TO TASTE

In a skillet, toast cumin seeds for 1 or 2 minutes until brown. Next you will mix cumin seeds, black beans, corn, red pepper, onion, cilantro, parsley, lime juice, olive oil, garlic, red pepper, tossing well. Cover and store in refrigerator. I serve with tortilla chips or Fritos.

Jane VanFossen

Grilled Parmesan Bread

In a small bowl combine butter and garlic and mix well (you may want to melt your butter and then mix) and set aside.

6 SLICES OF SOUR DOUGH BREAD OR ITALIAN BREAD

½ CUP OF BUTTER

2 GARLIC CLOVES

1 CUP OF SHREDDED PARMESAN

Place one side of your bread on grill until golden brown (2-4 min.) Then remove bread from grill and return to work area and spread butter mixture over top of each slice of bread. Next you want to sprinkle generously Parmesan cheese over top of butter spread. Now you are ready to place bread back on grill with butter and cheese facing on top. Cover grill and let cheese melt, about 2-4 min. Remove from grill.

Christensen Family

Chilled Strawberry Soup

7 CUPS SLICED FRESH STRAWBERRIES
2 CUPS HALF-AND-HALF
1 ½ CUPS SOUR CREAM
¾ CUP SIFTED POWDERED SUGAR
¼ CUP BALSAMIC VINEGAR
WHIPPED CREAM (OPTIONAL)
STRAWBERRY SLICES (OPTIONAL)
FRESH MINT SPRIGS (OPTIONAL)

In electric blender or food processor blend strawberries until smooth. Then place strawberry puree in large bowl. Next you blend half-and-half, sour cream, powdered sugar, and balsamic vinegar with a wire whisk until smooth. You must chill at least 2 hours. Personally I choose to garnish with a dollop of whipping cream, strawberry slice, and mint sprig.

Abbey Christensen

Cold Peach Soup

In your food processor blend peaches, wine, sugar, and a touch of honey. Next you will add water to desired consistency.

Gail Christensen

¾ CUP WHITE RHINE WINE

1 PACKAGE FROZEN PEACHES OR 2 CUPS FRESH PEACHES

SUGAR, HONEY, OR GRANULATED SUGAR SUBSTITUTE TO TASTE

Mary Elizabeth "Liz" Wood is Administrator of the Oklahoma Governor's Mansion.

The first couple with the Governor's Mansion staff. Left to right, Governor Mary Fallin, First Gentleman Wade Christensen, Karen Schwartz, Liz Wood, Toni Davis, and Chef Robin L. Obert.

Much of the grilling at the governor's mansion is done around the swimming pool, built in the shape of the State of Oklahoma. *Courtesy Roxanne Whited.*

The reflecting pond in the backyard of the Governor's Mansion. *Courtesty Roxanne Whited.*

The First Gentleman with his sister, Jane, and brothers Clay and Drew.

Wade's children, Brittiany, Alex, Adam, and Blake.

SIDE DISHES

Grilled Veggies

1 BUNCH ASPARAGUS (ABOUT 12 TO 14 STALKS), RINSED AND BOTTOMS SNAPPED OFF

2 ZUCCHINI, SLICED ON A DIAGONAL ¼ INCH THICK

4 JAPANESE EGGPLANTS, SLICED ON A DIAGONAL INTO ¼-INCH-THICK PIECES

2 RED BELL PEPPERS, SEEDED AND CUT INTO QUARTERS

1 LARGE YELLOW OR RED ONION, PEELED AND SLICED INTO ROUND ¼-INCH PIECES

3 TABLESPOONS EXTRA-VIRGIN OLIVE OIL

KOSHER SALT

FRESH OREGANO, FOR GARNISH

We always preheat an indoor or outdoor grill pan until hot. Brush vegetables with olive oil (you may use any combination of vegetables you like). You will want to add vegetables in separate batches because some vegetables cook quicker than others. After vegetables are grilled, arrange on platter and drizzle with extra virgin olive oil. Next you will sprinkle with Kosher salt and fresh oregano.

Wade & Mary

Mary's Aunt Barb Morrow and Jack Hays with the Governor and the First Gentleman.

Italian Zucchini Crescent Pie

4 CUPS THINLY SLICED UNPEELED ZUCCHINI

1 CUP CHOPPED ONION

½ CUP BUTTER

½ CUP PARSLEY OR 2 TABLESPOONS FLAKES

½ TEASPOON PEPPER

½ TEASPOON SALT

¼ TEASPOON GARLIC POWDER

¼ TEASPOON SWEET BASIL LEAVES

¼ TEASPOON OREGANO

2 EGGS, WELL BEATEN

8 OUNCES (2 CUPS) SHREDDED MOZZARELLA

1 (8 OUNCE) CAN PILLSBURY QUICK CRESCENT ROLLS

2 TEASPOONS PREPARED MUSTARD

Heat oven to 375 degrees. In skillet cook zucchini, onion, and butter until tender. Stir in parsley and seasonings. In a bowl, blend eggs and cheese. Add vegetable mixture. Separate dough into 8 triangles, place in ungreased 11-inch quiche pan or 8×12 baking dish. Press over bottom and up sides to form crust. Spread crust with mustard. Pour vegetables over evenly. Bake for 18-20 minutes. Let stand 10 minutes (If crust browns too fast, cover with foil the last 10 minutes.)

Barb Morrow

Scalloped Tomatoes

**6 MEDIUM TOMATOES PEELED AND CUT UP (2 POUNDS)
OR ONE 28 OUNCE CAN TOMATOES CUT UP**

1 CUP CELERY

½ CUP ONION

2 TABLESPOONS ALL PURPOSE FLOUR

1 TABLESPOON SUGAR

2 TABLESPOONS BUTTER OR MARGARINE

4 SLICES BREAD TOASTED

2 TABLESPOONS PARMESAN GRATED CHEESE

½ TEASPOON SALT

DASH PEPPER

In a sauce pan combine tomatoes, celery, and onion. Simmer covered about 10 minutes or until celery is tender. Combine flour, sugar, salt, and pepper. Stir in ½ cup water, add to tomatoes. Cook until thickened and bubbly. Cook 1 to 2 minutes more. Stir in butter until melted. Cut 3 slices toast into cubes, stir into tomato mixture. Pour into 1 1/2 quart casserole. Bake at 350 degrees for 30 minutes. Cut the remaining piece of toast into 4 triangles. Arrange triangles down center of tomato mixture, overlap slightly. Sprinkle with Parmesan cheese. Bake 20 minutes longer.

Mary Jo Copeland

Stuffed Tomatoes

4 RIPE MEDIUM TOMATOES
2 TABLESPOONS FINELY CHOPPED ONION
2 TABLESPOONS FINELY CHOPPED PARSLEY
½ CUP FINELY GRATED PARMESAN CHEESE
⅓ CUP BREAD CRUMBS
3 TABLESPOONS OLIVE OIL

Carefully cut top off tomatoes. Using spoon, carefully scoop out pulp and seeds. Save pulp, discard seeds. I use good part of tops. Coarsely chop the tomato pulp. Preheat oven to 350 degrees. In a small bowl combine tomato pulp onion, parsley, Parmesan cheese, bread crumbs, and oil. Spoon mixture into hollowed out tomatoes. Place tomatoes right side up in 8×8 baking dish and bake 15 minutes. Serve steaming hot.

Mary Jo Copeland

Slow Cooker Baked Beans

3 CUPS DRIED WHITE NAVY BEANS, SOAKED OVERNIGHT

1 ½ CUPS KETCHUP

1 ½ CUPS WATER

¼ CUP MOLASSES

1 VIDALIA OR SWEET ONION, CHOPPED

1 TABLESPOON GROUND MUSTARD

6 SLICES BACON, CHOPPED

1 CUP FIRMLY PACKED DARK BROWN SUGAR

KOSHER SALT – GROUND BLACK PEPPER

Drain beans, place in 4 quart slow cooker. Add ketchup, 1 ½ cups water, molasses, onion, mustard, bacon, brown sugar, salt, and pepper. Stir to combine. Cover and cook on low for 8 to 10 hours or on high 4 to 5 hours.

Barb Morrow

Alabama Scramble

Clean and cut or slice vegetables, dredging with corn meal, one vegetable at a time. Next you place one vegetable at a time in medium to hot oil. Push to side and brown next vegetable. Then fry all vegetables together, occasionally turning. Bake a pan of cornbread and you have a complete meal.

Jo Christensen

2 CUPS OKRA
1 CUP GREEN TOMATOES
2 CUPS YELLOW SQUASH
2 CUPS ZUCCHINI
½ CUP ONION
2 CUPS DICED POTATOES
SALT AND PEPPER TO TASTE
1 TO 2 CUPS OF CORN MEAL
OIL TO COVER BOTTOM OF FRYING SKILLET

Grilled Asparagus with Toasted Mustard Seed Vinaigrette

1 POUND ASPARAGUS
1 ½ TABLESPOONS CHAMPAGNE VINEGAR
1 ½ TABLESPOONS DIJON MUSTARD
2 TABLESPOONS PARSLEY (CHOPPED)
½ TEASPOON ONION POWDER
½ TEASPOON GARLIC POWDER
½ CUP OLIVE OIL
2 TEASPOONS MUSTARD SEEDS (TOASTED)

Toast mustard seeds in pan. Cover with splatter screen while constantly (and gently) shaking pan. Grill asparagus to desired doneness. Combine vinegar, Dijon, parsley, onion powder, and garlic powder. Mix well. Whisk in olive oil, adding a tablespoon at a time. Once fully blended drizzle over asparagus and then sprinkle toasted mustard seeds on top.

Chef Robin L. Obert

Tomato-Stuffed Yellow Squash

3 TO 4 MEDIUM-SIZE YELLOW SQUASH

¼ CUP CHOPPED ONION

2 GARLIC CLOVES, MINCED

2 TEASPOONS OLIVE OIL

3 PLUM TOMATOES, PEELED, SEEDED, AND DICED

1 TABLESPOON CHOPPED FRESH OREGANO

¼ TEASPOON SALT

¼ TEASPOON FRESHLY GROUND PEPPER

⅓ CUP FINE, DRY BREADCRUMBS

3 TABLESPOONS SHREDDED PARMESAN CHEESE

Boil squash in a saucepan for 5 minutes until tender; drain and plunge squash into ice water (this will stop the cooking process). Cut squash in half lengthwise; carefully scoop out seeds. Saute onion and garlic in skillet for 5 minutes. Next you will stir in tomato and remaining ingredients until thoroughly heated. Fold in bread crumbs and spoon mixture into squash shells. Sprinkle with cheese, placing on a baking sheet. Bake, covered at 375 degrees for 25 minutes.

Mary Jo Copeland

Summer Squash and Cherry Tomatoes in Basil Butter

1 POUND YELLOW SQUASH, THINLY SLICED
8 OUNCES CHERRY TOMATOES, HALVED
⅔ CUP BASIL BUTTER, DIVIDED

Sauté squash and tomato in 2 tablespoons Basil Butter in a large skillet over medium-high heat 10 minutes or until squash is tender. Serve with remaining Basil Butter.

BASIL BUTTER:
3 GARLIC CLOVES, MINCED
1 SHALLOT, MINCED
¾ CUP TIGHTLY PACKED FRESH BASIL LEAVES
½ CUP BUTTER OR MARGARINE, SOFTENED
FRESHLY GROUND PEPPER TO TASTE

Process all ingredients in a food processor until smooth, stopping once to scrape down sides. Cover and chill until ready to use.

Mary Jo Copeland

Grilled Sweet Potato Casserole

2 CUPS SWEET POTATOES
¾ CUP SUGAR
1 EGG (BEATEN)
½ TEASPOON VANILLA
¼ CUP BUTTER
⅛ TEASPOON NUTMEG
¼ CUP WALNUTS (TOASTED AND CHOPPED)
¼ CUP RAISINS
½ CUP JACK DANIELS
SALT TO TASTE

TOPPING:
1 CUP BROWN SUGAR
¼ CUP FLOUR
1 CUP PECANS (TOASTED AND CHOPPED)
¼ CUP + 2 TABLESPOONS BUTTER (MELTED)
½ TEASPOON CINNAMON
½ CUP BACON (COOKED UNTIL CRISPY/CHOPPED)

Grill whole sweet potatoes on low flame until thoroughly cooked. Allow to sit until cool enough to handle. Peel sweet potatoes and mash. In a pan combine Jack Daniels and raisins. Simmer until liquid is absorbed into the raisins. Combine white sugar, sweet potatoes, egg, butter, nutmeg, walnuts, and salt. Heat until butter is melted. Pour into a small casserole that has been coated with pan spray. Meanwhile, mix together brown sugar, flour, cinnamon, butter, and pecans. Sprinkle over potato mixture and finish with bacon. Bake at 350 degrees until cooked through, about 30 minutes.

Chef Robin L. Obert

Rameen and Gail Christensen.

Fried Green Beans

ITALIAN STYLE CUT GREEN BEANS, DRAINED
ONIONS, CHOPPED INTO LARGE PIECES
BACON
SEASONING SALT
PEPPER

Adjust the ingredients for the amount of beans you need. Fry bacon in large skillet. Remove, drain, and cut in pieces. Leave some bacon grease in the skillet and sauté the onions. Add the green beans and bacon to the onions in the skillet. Season with seasoning salt and pepper. Cook until soft. Can be prepared early and kept warm in a crock pot.

Rameen Christensen

Broccoli and Rice

- 7 OUNCE PACKAGE MINUTE RICE
- ½ CUP CHOPPED ONION
- ¼ POUND OLEO
- ¼ CUP CHOPPED CELERY
- 1 CUP MUSHROOM SOUP
- ½ CAN WATER
- 1 SMALL JAR CHEEZ WHIZ
- 1 PACKAGE CHOPPED BROCCOLI

Prepare rice as directed. Sauté onion and celery in oleo. Cook broccoli.

Combine all ingredients in casserole and bake 45 minutes at 350 degrees.

Nola Christensen

Barbecue Slaw

Combine sugar, ketchup, vinegar, and honey in a small saucepan, bringing to a boil until sugar dissolves. Pour warm mixture over cabbage, toss well. You must cover and chill at least 3 hours.

Mansion Staff

1 TEASPOON HONEY
⅓ CUP SUGAR
⅓ CUP KETCHUP
¼ CUP WHITE VINEGAR
11 CUPS SHREDDED CABBAGE
(ABOUT 1 MEDIUM CABBAGE)

Classic Potato Salad

3 POUNDS RED POTATOES OR YELLOW FINN POTATOES
2 CELERY RIBS, DICED
½ CUP CHOPPED SWEET PICKLES OR DILL PICKLES (YOUR PREFERENCE IN TASTE)
3 LARGE HARD-COOKED EGGS, SLICED
⅓ CUP WHITE CHOPPED ONION
2 GREEN ONIONS, CHOPPED
1 CUP MAYONNAISE
2 TABLESPOONS LEMON JUICE
SALT AND PEPPER TO TASTE
½ TEASPOON DRY MUSTARD (OPTIONAL)

Boil potatoes 25 minutes or until potatoes are tender. Drain very well and cool. Cube potatoes with or without peel. Next you will combine celery, pickles, eggs, and onions in a large bowl, tossing gently. In a small bowl combine mayonnaise, lemon juice, salt and pepper, and dry mustard (if desired).

Mary Fallin

Classic Stuffed Deviled Eggs

6 LARGE HARD-COOKED EGGS

¼ CUP MAYONNAISE

1 TABLESPOON SWEET PICKLE RELISH OR DILL RELISH (YOUR PREFERENCE)

½ TEASPOON PREPARED MUSTARD

SALT AND PEPPER TO TASTE

PAPRIKA

6 PIMENTO-STUFFED OLIVES, HALVED

After boiling eggs, slice in half lengthwise. You must carefully remove yolks and mash yolks with mayonnaise. Next you will add relish, mustard, salt, and pepper, mixing well. Spoon mixture into egg whites. Sprinkle paprika on top and garnish with an olive half.

Jo Christensen

GETTING GRILLED BY WADE CHRISTENSEN

Mexican Deviled Eggs

6 HARD-COOKED EGGS
1 ½ TABLESPOONS SOUR CREAM
1 TABLESPOON SALSA
1 TABLESPOON GREEN ONIONS
3 ½ TABLESPOONS CHEDDAR CHEESE

Slice eggs in half lengthwise and remove yolks. Mash egg yolks with sour cream and salsa. Spoon mixture into egg whites and sprinkle with finely chopped green onions and finely grated cheddar cheese.

Ronnye Perry Sharp

Governor Mary Fallin's grandmother, Ina Duggan, from Tecumseh, OK.

SWEETS
FOR THE SWEET

Coconut Cream Cake

½ CUP SHORTENING

½ CUP MARGARINE

2 CUPS SUGAR

5 EGGS SEPARATED

2 CUPS SIFTED FLOUR

1 TEASPOON SODA

1 CUP BUTTERMILK

1 (7 OUNCE) CAN FLAKE COCONUT
   ⅔ CUP FOR CAKE
   1 CUP FOR FILLING

In a large bowl or mixer blend shortening and margarine together at high speed. Add sugar gradually and beat until fluffy. Add egg yolks one at a time, beating well after each addition.

Sift flour and soda together. Add alternately with buttermilk. Beginning and ending with flour mixture. Add ⅔ cup coconut to cake mixture (batter). Beat egg whites until stiff peaks form. Fold in batter. Pour into 3 greased and floured 9 in cake pans. Bake in 350 degree oven 25 to 30 minutes. Cool, frost with cream filling.

FILLING:

1 STICK MARGARINE, SOFTENED

1 (8 OUNCE) PACKAGE PHILADELPHIA
   CREAM CHEESE SOFTENED

1 BOX POWDERED SUGAR

CREAMED TOGETHER

Mix well. Put between and on top and sides of layers. Sprinkle 1 small can coconut on top and sides of cake.

Ina Duggan, grandmother of Mary Fallin

Strawberry Cake

1 BOX WHITE CAKE MIX
½ CUP WATER
½ CUP STRAWBERRIES & JUICE
1 SMALL BOX STRAWBERRY JELLO
1 CUP OIL
5 EGGS

Mix on low speed until blended. Mix on medium speed 2 minutes. Pour into prepared pan. Bake at 325 degrees until tester indicates cake is done. Cool and ice with strawberry glaze below.

Mix until smooth. Add water if necessary. Pour over cake.

June & Everett Adams

STRAWBERRY GLAZE
2 POUNDS POWDERED SUGAR
1/8 TEASPOON SALT
1 (10 OUNCE) PACKAGE FROZEN STRAWBERRIES, THAWED
¼ CUP VEGETABLE OIL

Strawberry-Fudge Brownies

1 BOX (1 POUND 2.3 OUNCE) BETTY CROCKER FUDGE BROWNIE MIX
¼ CUP WATER
⅔ CUP VEGETABLE OIL
3 EGGS
1 ½ CUPS FROZEN STRAWBERRIES, THAWED, DRAINED
½ CUP CHOPPED PECANS
½ CUP CHOPPED ALMONDS
½ CUP FLAKED COCONUT
½ CUP BETTY CROCKER RICH & CREAMY CHOCOLATE FROSTING (FROM 1 POUND CONTAINER)

Grease the bottom of 9×13 pan with cooking oil or spray. In a medium bowl, stir your brownie mix, water, oil, and eggs, scraping bowl occasionally, adding your strawberries. Blend well. Next you will blend in pecans, almonds, and coconut. Spread batter in pan and bake at 325 degrees for 45 minutes. Cool completely before frosting. In a small bowl microwave frosting about 15 to 20 seconds. Then drizzle frosting over brownies.

Brittiany Christensen

Cream Cheese Bars

2 CANS CROISSANT ROLL DOUGH
2 (8 OUNCE) BOXES OF CREAM CHEESE
1 ½ CUPS SUGAR-DIVIDED
2 TEASPOONS VANILLA
1 STICK BUTTER
2 TEASPOONS CINNAMON

Soften 2 boxes of cream cheese in microwave for a minute or two. Then stir in 1 cup sugar and 2 teaspoons of vanilla. Next you will melt a stick of butter in microwave. Stir the remaining sugar (½ cup) and 2 teaspoons of cinnamon and set aside. In a 9x13 pan lay out one can of refrigerated croissant rolls, covering the bottom of the pan. Spread your cream cheese mixture over rolls evenly. Next you will lay out the second can of rolls on top of filling, covering the cream cheese mixture. Finally you will top with the butter and sugar mixture. Bake at 350 degrees for 25 to 30 minutes. Cool and refrigerate in pan overnight.

Variations:

For chocolate cream cheese squares I add 1-2 tablespoons of cocoa to the cream cheese mixture and instead of cinnamon on the topping I add a teaspoon of cocoa.

Jane VanFossen

Lemon Bars

¾ CUP BUTTER, SOFT
1 ½ CUPS + 3 TABLESPOONS FLOUR
½ CUP POWDERED SUGAR
JUICE OF LEMON
1 ½ CUPS SUGAR
3 EGGS, BEATEN

FROSTING
JUICE 1 LEMON
1 TEASPOON LEMON RIND
3 TABLESPOONS BUTTER MELTED
2 CUPS POWDERED SUGAR
MIX AND POUR WHILE HOT OVER BARS

Mix butter and 1 ½ cups flour and powdered sugar. Press in 8x11 pan for the crust. Bake 350 degrees for 20 minutes. Mix sugar, lemon juice, eggs, and 3 tablespoons flour. Pour over crust and bake 20 minutes.

Erica Miles

Chocolate Trifle

1 (19.8 OUNCE) PACKAGE FUDGE BROWNIE MIX

¼ CUP COFFEE FLAVORED LIQUOR

1 (3.9 OUNCE) PACKAGE CHOCOLATE FUDGE INSTANT PUDDING MIX

8 (14 OUNCE) TOFFEE-FLAVORED CANDY BARS, CRUSHED

1 (10.8 OUNCE) CONTAINER COOL WHIP

Prepare brownie mix and bake it as directed on box in a 9x13 pan. Prick top of warm brownies about 1 inch apart. I use the handle of a wooden spoon. Brush with coffee liquor. Cool and crumble into small pieces. Prepare pudding according to package directions–omit chilling procedure. Place half of the brownies in bottom of a 3 quart glass trifle bowl. Layer with half of the pudding, crushed candy, and whipped topping. Repeat layers with remaining brownies, pudding, candy, and whipped topping. I like to top it off with chocolate curls made with a Hershey bar and a carrot peeler. Yum-Yum.

Jane VanFossen

Peach Ice Cream

4 EGGS
1 ½ CUPS SUGAR, MAYBE A LITTLE MORE
1 ½ CUPS CREAM
1 CUP HALF-AND-HALF
5 TO 6 PEACHES, PEELED AND MASHED
2 TEASPOONS ALMOND EXTRACT
1 TEASPOON VANILLA

Mix above ingredients. Pour into ice cream freezer container and fill to line with milk. Freeze according to your freezer directions.

Rachel and Jane VanFossen

Chocolate Pie

Mix sugar, flour, cocoa, egg yolks, and milk. Cook until thick. Add margarine and vanilla; Cool. Pour into crust.

Arlene Grimsley

1 CUP SUGAR
3 TABLESPOONS FLOUR
3 TABLESPOONS COCOA
2 OR 3 EGG YOLKS
2 CUPS MILK
2 TABLESPOONS MARGARINE
1 TEASPOON VANILLA
1 BAKED PIE CRUST

Oklahoma's Best Pecan Pie

5 EGG YOLKS
1 CUP SUGAR
1 CUP WHITE KARO SYRUP
3 TABLESPOONS BUTTER
1 ¼ CUPS BROKEN PECAN MEATS
5 EGG WHITES, WELL BEATEN
VANILLA TO TASTE

Cream butter, sugar, and egg yolks. Add syrup, vanilla, and pecans and stir well. Fold in egg whites. Pour mixture into unbaked pastry shell and bake slowly at 325 for 1 hour until custard-like in consistency. Serve with ice cream and a few pecans sprinkled over the top, or whipped cream.

EXCELLENT PIE CRUST:

2 CUPS FLOUR
½ TEASPOON SALT
⅓ CUP BUTTER
⅓ CUP WHITE VEGETABLE SHORTENING
ICE WATER (ABOUT 1/3 CUP)

Mix salt into flour. Work both shortenings into flour with pastry mixer or by crossing two knives against each other. Bits of shortening should be pea-sized. Moisten dough with ice water by stirring with a fork. Pat into 2 balls (for 2 crusts), wrap in wax paper, and chill thoroughly. This dough handles easily and bakes very well.

Ronnye Perry Sharp

Strawberry Bavarian

1 (3 OUNCE) PACKAGE STRAWBERRY GELATIN

1 CUP BOILING WATER

1 CUP SLICED, SWEETENED, FROZEN STRAWBERRIES WITH JUICE, DO NOT DRAIN

1 CUP HEAVY CREAM, WHIPPED (CAN USE SMALL TUB OF COOL WHIP)

Pour boiling water over gelatin in bowl, stirring until gelatin is dissolved. Stir strawberries and syrup into dissolved gelatin. Refrigerate mixture until almost set. Beat gelatin until foamy. Add whipped cream and chill until firm.

PIE CRUST:

2 CUPS FLOUR

1 CUP CRISCO

1 TEASPOON SALT

½ CUP FLOUR

½ CUP WATER

2 TEASPOONS HONEY OR KARO

Mix the 2 cups of flour, Crisco, and salt. In another bowl, mix the ½ cup flour, water, and honey or Karo. Add to first mixture.

Nola Christensen

Pink Lemonade Pie

2 CUPS CRUSHED VANILLA WAFERS

1 EGG WHITE

2 ½ TABLESPOONS BUTTER, MELTED AND
    COOLED SLIGHTLY

2 (14 OUNCE) CANS SWEETENED CONDENSED MILK

8 EGG YOLKS

1 CUP + 2 TABLESPOONS FRESH LEMON JUICE

PINK FOOD COLORING PASTE

2 CUPS HEAVY WHIPPING CREAM

½ CUP CONFECTIONERS' SUGAR

Preheat oven to 350 degrees. In a medium bowl, stir together crushed vanilla wafers, egg white, and butter. Press into a 10 inch pie plate. Bake for 10 minutes or until lightly browned. Cool completely. In a large bowl, whisk together milk, egg yolks, and lemon juice. Tint mixture to reach desired color. Pour into prepared crust. Bake for 20 to 25 minutes. Cool. Chill. Spread on whipping cream.

Rachel and Haley VanFossen

Lemon Party Pie

1 ½ CUPS FLOUR

⅔ CUP MARGARINE OR BUTTER

¾ CUP CHOPPED PECANS

2 CUPS WHIPPED TOPPING, DIVIDED

1 (8 OUNCE) PACKAGE CREAM CHEESE

½ CUP POWDERED SUGAR

2 SMALL BOXES LEMON
    INSTANT PUDDING

3 CUPS MILK

Work margarine into flour and add pecans and press into 9x13 pan. Bake at 350 degrees for 25 minutes. Cool. Mix together 1 ½ cups whipped topping, cream cheese, and powdered sugar. Place mixture over crust. Mix 2 boxes of pudding with the 3 cups of milk. Beat until thick. Place over cream cheese mixture. Top with remaining whipped topping. Chill. Fantastic!

Kimmy Christensen

Blackberry Cobbler

FILLING:
7 CUPS BLACKBERRIES
½ CUP SUGAR
1 TABLESPOON ALL-PURPOSE FLOUR
2 TEASPOONS LEMON ZEST
PINCH OF SALT

TOPPING:
1¼ CUPS ALL-PURPOSE FLOUR
⅓ CUP SUGAR
2 TEASPOONS BAKING POWDER
½ TEASPOON GROUND CINNAMON
¼ TEASPOON SALT
1 LARGE EGG YOLK, BEATEN, AT ROOM TEMPERATURE
½ CUP BUTTERMILK
6 TABLESPOONS UNSALTED BUTTER, MELTED
½ TEASPOON PURE VANILLA EXTRACT

You will lightly grease a glass pie plate. In a large bowl, gently toss blackberries with sugar, flour, lemon zest, and salt until blended. You will pour mixture into prepared baking dish and set aside. Next for your topping stir together flour, sugar, baking powder, cinnamon, and salt. In another bowl whisk together your egg yolk, buttermilk, butter, and vanilla. Using a rubber spatula, gently fold in your wet ingredients with the dry ingredients until forming a soft dough. Drop heaping spoonfuls of the topping over the fruit filling. Bake at 375 degrees for 45 minutes. Serve warm with a scoop of vanilla ice cream.

Rameen Christensen

Peach Cobbler

6 LARGE PEACHES
⅓ CUP SUGAR
1 STICK (1/2 CUP) BUTTER
1 CUP FLOUR
1 CUP SUGAR
⅔ CUP MILK
1 TABLESPOON BAKING POWDER

Peel and slice peaches; sprinkle with ⅓ cup sugar and let sit until juice forms. Melt butter and add 1 cup flour, 1 cup sugar, milk, baking powder, and salt; stir until smooth. Place in a 9x9 square. Put peaches and their juice on top of the crust; bake in a 350 degree oven uncovered for 1 hour. Serve with ice cream. Yum.

Abbey Christensen

Peach and Pineapple Sorbet

3 PEACHES, PEELED AND DICED
1 ½ TABLESPOONS ORANGE JUICE
½ CUP DICED PINEAPPLE
½ CUP SIMPLE SYRUP

Blend your peaches and orange juice in a food processor until smooth. Next you will add your pineapple puree until smooth. Add your simple syrup and pour entire mixture into an ice cream freezer; make and freeze.

Rachel and Haley VanFossen

Strawberry Frozen Delight

COMBINE:
1 CUP FLOUR
½ CUP MELTED BUTTER
¼ CUP BROWN SUGAR
1 CUP CHOPPED PECANS

Mix and spread on jelly roll pan; bake at 350 for 20 minutes, stirring every 5 minutes. Watch so that it doesn't burn. In a large mixing bowl, combine and beat at high speed for 20 minutes:

1 CUP SUGAR
2 LARGE EGG WHITES
2 TEASPOONS LEMON JUICE
1 (10 OUNCE) FROZEN STRAWBERRIES, THAWED, INCLUDING SYRUP

Whip and fold in ½ pint whipping cream and spread half of nut mixture on bottom of 9x13 Pyrex dish. Spread strawberry mixture next and finish by covering with nut mixture. Cover with foil and put in the freezer until frozen. Can make several days in advance and leave in freezer until ready to serve. May garnish with a dollop of whipping cream and a strawberry, if desired.

Erica Miles

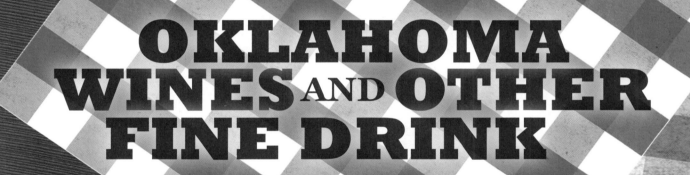

OKLAHOMA WINES AND OTHER FINE DRINK

Award-winning Oklahoma wines.

Wine Country

It was natural for European settlers in pre-statehood Oklahoma to plant grapes to produce their own wine as their forefathers had done in the Old Country. Much of the wine was made from a native species of wild grape, Vitis Doaniana, named for a Texas panhandle judge who found grapes for his wine making in Indian Territory.

Even before the Land Run of 1889, Edward B. Fairchild built the state's first wine vault on land in present northeast Oklahoma City where television antennas have dotted the landscape for the past half century. In 1884, Fairchild, from a prominent winemaking family in upstate New York, used native sandstone and built a wine vault over a natural spring. The 14-foot-by-41-foot vault still stands nearly 130 years later as Oklahoma City's oldest extant structure.

Fairchild planted 1,500 fruit trees and grapes. He built a wooden windmill with five-foot blades to pump water from the spring into canals he dug to water the orchard. When the site was rediscovered in the 1970s, the canal system still was operational. George Shirk, the former Oklahoma City mayor and president of the

GETTING GRILLED BY WADE CHRISTENSEN

Oklahoma Historical Society, discovered the remnants of the Fairchild Winery in a garbage dump. The wine vault was restored and used for regular meetings of the Oklahoma Wine and Rasslin' Society. In 1974, the vault was placed on the National Register of Historic Places.

At peak production, Fairchild produced 5,500 gallons of wine annually, primarily from Concord and Wisconsin grapes. As Oklahoma City grew, Fairchild served his wine in several restaurants in which he had an interest.

Then, prohibition put Fairchild and other wineries out of business. As Oklahoma entered the Union as the 46th state in November, 1907, the state constitution prohibited the sale of alcoholic beverages. The 1910 federal census showed Oklahoma with more than 4,000 acres of vineyard, placing it eighth among all the states. Oklahoma had become a splendid grape-

The Fairchild Wine Vault in northeast Oklahoma City.

growing region, but the politics of the time put wine production on hold. Even though court decisions allowed churches to buy wine for sacrament purposes, the market was not sufficient to sustain Oklahoma wineries.

Bootleggers, making moonshine whiskey, home beer brewers, and winemakers flourished through the decades of prohibition, but voters did not officially eliminate prohibition until 1959. Bootleg whiskey and wine became big business in the 1920s and 1930s as oil booms brought thousands of rowdy workers to small towns that blossomed overnight. Lawmen could not keep up with the illegal flow of strong drink. Oklahoma's favorite son, humorist Will Rogers, said, "Oklahomans will vote dry as long as they can stagger to the polls."

A variety of wine grapes grow well in Oklahoma.

In the 1940s Professor Herman Heinrichs began vineyard development at Oklahoma A & M and created a hybrid grape, the Rubaiyat. In the 1970s, Governor David Hall sponsored a viticulture initiative in southeast Oklahoma to provide employment for welfare recipients. After George Shirk helped revitalize the Fairchild wine vault, the Fairchild

The Chapel Creek Winery in El Reno.

Wine Society was founded. The Dos Okies Winery used the Rubaiyat grape to produce wine. In 1982, Dwayne and Susie Pool opened the Cimarron Cellars Winery in Caney, the first winery to be open continuously into the twenty-first century.

The Oklahoma Grape Growers and Wine Makers Association was founded in 1994 by Max Knotts, Robert Bartunck, and George Girard. The first meeting of the group was held at the Dos Okies Winery in 1995.

In 2000, voters approved State Question 688 that allowed Oklahoma wineries to sell their wines directly to retail liquor stores and restaurants, but a federal judge declared the mandate unconstitutional. In 2008,

State Question 743 was approved by 79 percent of Oklahoma voters. It allowed all wineries under 10,000-gallon capacity to sell directly to liquor stores and restaurants. The uncertain status of the law causes many wineries to sell only on-site. In 2012, the Oklahoma Supreme Court cleared the way for a proposed constitutional amendment that would allow wine to be sold in Oklahoma grocery stores, if approved by voters in the future.

In the past 25 years, the number of wineries in the nation, including Oklahoma, has exploded. Cultivation of wine grapes gives small landowners the opportunity to use less fertile soil that might not be suitable for other types of agriculture. In 1996, there were only two wineries in the state. Today there are dozens, adding to the charm of Oklahoma as a tourist destination. Wineries are located throughout the state with the exception of the Panhandle.

Oklahoma wineries range from small family-operated facilities with friendly tasting rooms to large rural attractions with pleasant pastoral views over an expanse of vineyards. Wine aficionados enjoy sunny evenings at wineries listening to live jazz, strolling through picturesque vineyards with glass in hand, or lingering over the finest gourmet meal with a bottle of a newly-discovered Oklahoma vintage wine.

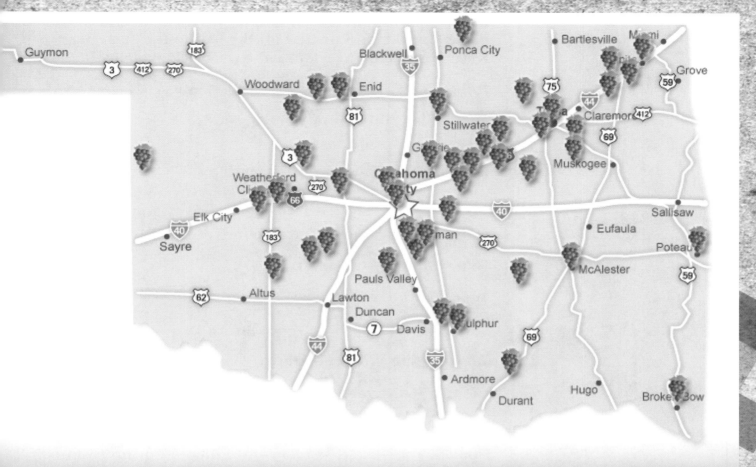

Oklahoma wineries are spread throughout the state.

WINERIES AND VINEYARDS IN OKLAHOMA

Members of the Oklahoma Grape Growers and Wine Makers Association and attractions from www.travelok.com.

Northeastern Oklahoma

Nuyaka Creek Winery—Winery and vineyard is located deep in the woods at the intersection of Okmulgee, Creek, and Okfuskee counties in Nuyaka, about 45 minutes south of Tulsa.

StableRidge Vineyards—This winery opened in 2004, on Historic Route 66 in Stroud. The tasting room was made from a restored 1902 Catholic Church.

Stone Bluff Cellars—Overlooks the Tulsa skyline and offers wine tasting and gift shop five miles north of Haskell.

Lavender Hill Farm and Winery—Haskell.

Tidal School Vineyards—Drumright.

Summerside Vineyards, Winery & Inn—Vineyard with bed & breakfast. Located off the Vinita I-44 exit near Ketchum Cove on Grand Lake O' the Cherokees.

Roberdes Family Vineyards and Winery—Claremore.

Oak Hills Winery and Vineyards—Near Grand Lake in Chelsea.

Hickory Hill Vineyard—Okemah.

Lakeside Vineyard—Afton.

Gander Way Vineyard and Winery—Skiatook.

Grape Ranch—Okemah.

Woodland Park Winery—Stillwater.

Girouard Vines Winery—Tulsa.

Blue Coyote Winery—Adair.

Central Oklahoma

Sparks Vineyard & Winery—In Lincoln County, amidst the beautiful country setting of Sparks.

Moonfeathers Winery—Tasting room, gift shop, production room, and fields of grapevines in historic Guthrie.

Urban Wineworks at the Plaza—Oklahoma City.

Chapel Creek Winery—El Reno.

Redbud Ridge Vineyard and Winery—Norman.

Clauren Ridge Vineyard and Winery—Edmond.

Canadian River Vineyards & Winery—Seven acres of vineyards in Lexington.

Willow Ponds Vineyards—Lexington.

Parsons Vineyard and Winery—Shawnee.

Tidal School Vineyards—Oklahoma's largest automated wine bottling line. Tasting room is located off Highway 16, two miles south of Drumright.

GreenField Vineyard and Winery—Four miles northeast of Chandler.

Woodland Park Vineyards and Winery—A small family-owned Oklahoma winery in Stillwater.

Tres Suenos Vineyards and Winery—Luther.

Deer Creek Vineyard—Award-winning winery in Edmond.

Nellis Vineyards—Edmond

Redstone Vineyards and Winery—Luther.

Rosebrook Vineyards—Oklahoma City.

Smokin' Grapes Vineyard—Oklahoma City.

Farfalla Winery—Yukon.

Sand Hills Vineyards—El Reno.

Strebel Creek Vineyard—Oklahoma City.

Put a Cork In It—Oklahoma City's Bricktown.

The Grape Junction—Stroud.

Native Spirits Winery—Norman.

Territory Cellars—Stroud.

Northwestern Oklahoma

Indian Creek Village Winery—Ringwood.

Robert Bartunek Winery—More than two acres of vineyard in Enid.

Turkey Creek Vineyards—European-style wines made from grapes grown on the homestead near Durham.

Whirlwind Winery—Watonga.

Base Vines and Cattle—Geary.

Plain View Winery—Lahoma.

Prairie Wind Winery—Burns Flat.

Prairie Rattler Winery—Shidler.

Plymouth Valley Cellars—Fairview.

Southern Oklahoma

Cimarron Cellars—The oldest operating winery in the

state, located 18 miles northeaset of Durant.

Woods & Waters Winery—Six varieties of grapes grown on eight acres at Anadarko.

Girls Gone Wine—Hochatown winery north of Broken Bow, offering local wine tasting near the scenic Mountain Fork River.

Black Sheep Winery and Vineyards—Poteau.

Sunset Ridge Vineyard—Duncan.

Triple R Vineyard—Mangum.

Waddell Vineyard and Wine Cellar—Ada.

Quartz Mountain Winery—Lone Wolf.

The Range Winery—Anadarko.

Wakefield Winery—Stuart.

Legends Vineyard and Winery—Lindsay.

Washita Valley Winery—Sulphur.

Windmill Winery—Roosevelt.

Whispering Meadows Vineyard and Winery—McAlester.

The Rusty Nail Winery—Sulphur.

BREWING OKLAHOMA BEER

The American brewing industry began in 1587 when Virginia colonists brewed ale from corn. Within the next two decades, advertisements appeared in London newspapers beckoning brewers to the Virginia Colony. In 1612, two Dutchmen opened the first brewery in the New World on the southern tip of New Amsterdam (Manhattan).

By 1867, nearly 4,000 breweries were in operation in America, producing six-million barrels of beer annually. Citizens who were opposed to consumption of alcoholic beverages began organizing prohibition efforts. Twenty three states were dry by World War I as prohibitionists gained power and influence. In 1919, the 18th Amendment to the United States Constitution mandated national prohibition. Americans continued to drink beer, but had to do so illegally, or revert to homebrewing.

In 1933, when the 21st Amendment repealed prohibition, 3.2 % beer came to Oklahoma. Even though Oklahoma was still a dry state, 3.2 % beer was defined as a "nonintoxicating beverage." Flour-mill magnate John Kroutil and Gustave Streich started the Progress Brewing Company in Oklahoma City in 1933, one of only three post-prohibition brewing licenses issued in Oklahoma. The brewery was sold to Lone Star Beer in 1959.

Brewing in Tulsa began in 1938 when the Ahrens Brewing Company began brewing its Ranger Beer line. Ahrens went bankrupt in 1940 and brewing did not return to Tulsa until the 1990s when the Cherry Street Brewing Company and the Tulsa Brewing Company attempted the brewpub model—operating a restaurant and bar as well as tending to brewing operations. In 2008, Marshall Brewing Company ushered in a new era of brewing in Tulsa.

Choc beer, short for Choctaw Indian beer, is Oklahoma's oldest beer. In Indian Territory, residents

TheBeerCanGuide.com

Progress Beer was brewed in Oklahoma City beginning in 1933.

of southeastern Oklahoma, Choctaw country, fermented malted barley and hops, a "home brew" that was flavored to the maker's taste, often with fruits or other ingredients. Pete Prichard, an Italian immigrant, began peddling choc beer to coal miners after his leg was crushed in a mining accident in 1916. In 1925 he formally opened Pete's Place in Krebs.

For more than a century, choc beer was brewed in kitchens, garages, and barns and secretly sold to known and trusted customers. At the end of the twentieth century, Pete's Place legally sold choc beer as a specialty item. For most of the state's history, it was illegal to brew choc beer without a license, although its brewing remained a popular pastime. In 2010, a law was passed by the legislature and signed by Governor Brad Henry that made brewing beer for personal consumption legal. Home production of wine and cider for personal consumption already was legal.

Oklahoma's alcohol laws prevent brewpubs, restaurants with an on premise brewery, from brewing beer with an alcohol content greater than 3.2% by weight or 4% by volume. Also, any beer above 3.2%

Modern-brewed choc beer.

The Oklahoma Craft Beer Festival held in Oklahoma City's Bricktown each May is the state's largest beer-tasting event and celebrates the Oklahoma brewing industry. Nearly 50 in-state and out-of-state breweries present 200 beers at the festival.

Oklahoma accounts for 55 percent of the 3.2 % beer sold in the United States. The rest is sold in Utah, Kansas, Colorado, Minnesota, and Missouri. Oklahoma is 30th in the country in per-capita beer consumption. New Hampshire residents drink the most, per capita, and Utah citizens drink the least.

Oklahoma has 16 breweries and brewpubs, 45 beer wholesalers, and nearly 7,000 beer retailers. Beer sales add nearly $70-million excise and sales tax revenues in the state. By the end of the twentieth century, more than 500 breweries were in operation in the nation. In addition, hundreds of micro-breweries were established.

alcohol must be sold unrefrigerated in licensed liquor stores.

In 2012, OKCity Brewing Company established a cooperative of three breweries to spur the growing Oklahoma craft beer market, which has expanded rapidly in recent years. Redbud Brewing, Anthem Brewing, and Black Mesa Brewing have joined the cooperative which allows individual brewers to rent time on the towering stainless steel brew kettles and fermenting tanks, keg their product, and ship to market.

The proliferation of craft brewers in Oklahoma projects a positive image for out-of-town visitors. For managers of restaurants and drinking establishments, the availability of a variety of local beers is a plus.

GETTING GRILLED BY WADE CHRISTENSEN

Oklahoma Breweries

Battered Boar Brewing Company - Edmond

Choc Beer Company - Krebs

COOP Ale Works - Oklahoma City

Huebert Brewing Company - Oklahoma City

Marshall Brewing Company - Tulsa

Redbud Brewing Company - Oklahoma City

Mustang Brewing Company — Mustang

Barley Field Brewing Company — Tulsa

T. Paul's Beer Company — Tulsa

Black Mesa Brewing Company — Oklahoma City

Anthem Brewing Company — Oklahoma City

Oklahoma Brewpubs

Bricktown Brewery Restaurant & Pub - Oklahoma City

Belle Isle Restaurant & Brewing Company - Oklahoma City

Coach's Brewhouse - Norman

Pete's Place - Krebs

Royal Bavaria - Moore

Interurban Brewpub — Norman

Norman Brewing — Norman

Tulsa Brewing — Tulsa

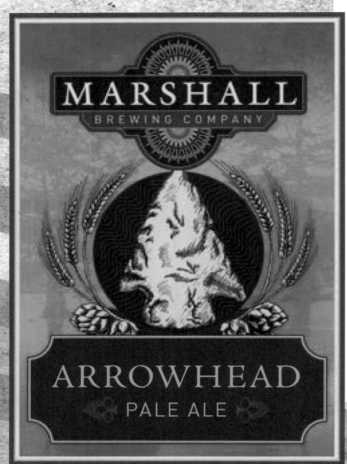

Taste of Bricktown features the finest of wines and beer at restaurants in the area.

The art of brewing local beer has grown in Oklahoma since the beginning of the new millennium.

Beer Can Chicken

1 (4-POUND) WHOLE CHICKEN
2 TABLESPOONS VEGETABLE OIL
2 TABLESPOONS SALT
1 TEASPOON BLACK PEPPER
3 TABLESPOONS OF YOUR FAVORITE
   DRY SPICE RUB
1 CAN BEER

This has to be one of Oklahoma grillers' favorite novelty recipes to prepare.

Remove neck and giblets from chicken and discard. Rinse chicken inside and out, and pat dry with paper towels. Rub chicken lightly with oil then rub inside and out with salt, pepper, and dry rub. Set aside. Open beer can and take several gulps (make them big gulps so that the can is half full). Place beer can on a solid surface. Grabbing a chicken leg in each hand, plunk the bird cavity over the beer can. Transfer the bird-on-a-can to your grill and place in the center of the grate, balancing the bird on the 2 legs and the can like a tripod. Cook the chicken over medium-high, indirect heat (i.e. no coals or burners on directly under the bird), with the grill cover on, for approximately 1 ¼ hours or until the internal temperature registers 165 degrees F in the breast area and 180 degrees F in the thigh, or until the thigh juice runs clear when stabbed with a sharp knife. Remove from grill and let rest for 10 minutes before carving.

Beer Brats

1 DOZEN BRATS
BEER, TO COVER
1 MEDIUM LARGE SWEET ONION
2 OUNCES (1/2 STICK) BUTTER

This recipe is a tailgate favorite. Place brats in a Dutch oven with onions and butter, cover the brats with beer. Bring to a boil and reduce to simmer until brats are cooked.

Remove brats and set aside beer mixture. Grill brats until golden brown and return to beer mixture until ready to serve. Serve brats on fresh baked brat buns with sauerkraut, onions, green peppers, ketchup, and/or mustard.

Beer Bread

3 CUPS FLOUR (SIFTED)
3 TEASPOONS BAKING POWDER
    (OMIT IF USING SELF-RISING FLOUR)
1 TEASPOON SALT
    (OMIT IF USING SELF-RISING FLOUR)
¼ CUP SUGAR
1 (12 OUNCE) CAN BEER
½ CUP MELTED BUTTER
    (¼ CUP WILL DO JUST FINE)

Women and men across the country have been preparing this easy recipe for years. Preheat oven to 375 degrees. Mix dry ingredients and beer. Pour into a greased loaf pan. Pour melted butter over mixture. Bake 1 hour, remove from pan, and cool for at least 15 minutes.

Updated Notes:

This recipe makes a very hearty bread with a crunchy, buttery crust. If you prefer a softer crust, like a traditional bread, mix the butter into the batter instead of pouring it over the top. Sifting flour for bread recipes is a must-do. Most people just scoop the 1 cup measure in the flour canister and level it off. That compacts the flour and will turn your bread into a "hard biscuit" as some have described. That's because they aren't sifting their flour! If you do not have a sifter, use a spoon to spoon the flour in the 1 cup measure. Try it once the "correct" way and you will see an amazing difference in the end product.

Orange Julius

This is a family favorite and very simple. Just combine all ingredients in blender and serve this delightfully refreshing beverage.

Erica Miles

1 SMALL CAN ORANGE JUICE
1 CUP HALF AND HALF
1 CUP WATER
½ CUP SUGAR OR SUGAR SUBSTITUTE
½ TEASPOON VANILLA
ICE CUBES

Pineapple-Orange Sangria

1 750-ML BOTTLE DRY RIESLING
1 CUP PEACH VODKA
1 CUP CANNED PINEAPPLE JUICE
¾ CUP APRICOT NECTAR
1 SMALL NAVEL ORANGE, QUARTERED LENGTHWISE AND THINLY SLICED
1 CUP PINEAPPLE TID-BITS
CLUB SODA

Stir wine, vodka, pineapple juice, and apricot nectar in large pitcher. You will add fruit to mixture and refrigerate at least 2 hours. Serve over ice and top-off each glass with a splash of club soda.

Mansion Staff

Lime Margaritas

2 CUPS ICE CUBES

1 CUP SUGAR SUBSTITUTE (RECOMMENDED: SPLENDA)

¾ CUP WATER

5 OUNCES TEQUILA

2 LEMONS, JUICED

2 LIMES, JUICED

GARNISH:

COARSE MARGARITA-STYLE SALT, AS NEEDED

LEMON SLICES, FOR GARNISH

LIME SLICES, FOR GARNISH

4 OLD-FASHIONED GLASSES

You will place all ingredients in a blender on high until smooth, (perhaps 1-2 minutes). Special secret: instead of water run a lemon slice around the rims to dampen glasses, then dip in a small plate of salt to coat. Pour margarita into glasses. Garnish with lime slice.

Mansion Staff

Fresh Strawberry Margaritas

4 CUPS FRESH STRAWBERRIES

2 ½ CUPS CRUSHED ICE

½ CUP TEQUILA-LIME

¾ CUP FRESH LIME JUICE

⅓ CUP SUGAR

3 TABLESPOONS CORINTREAU

This is such a delicious and easy recipe to prepare. Mix all ingredients in blender. Rim a cocktail glass with lime juice and dip rim on plate of salt. Pour margarita and garnish with strawberry.

Mansion Staff

Frozen Peach Margarita

Add the salt to a small-rimmed plate and ¼ cup water to another plate. Dip the rims of the glasses into the water then the salt. Set aside. Add the nectar, tequila, sweetened lime juice, liqueur, fresh lime juice, and peaches to a blender. Puree until smooth and serve immediately in the salt-rimmed glasses.

Chef Robin L. Obert

¼ OUNCE KOSHER SALT

¾ OUNCE PEACH NECTAR

¾ CUP TEQUILA

¼ OUNCE SWEETENED LIME JUICE, SUCH AS ROSE'S LIME JUICE

¼ CUP ORANGE-FLAVORED LIQUEUR, SUCH AS CORINTREAU

JUICE OF 1 LIME

1 (16-OUNCE) BAG FROZEN PEACHES

OKLAHOMA BBQ SMOKES THE COMPETITION

Some barbecue connoisseurs believe Memphis, Kansas City, or Fort Worth reign supreme in the art of grilling or barbecuing. However, facts prove otherwise. In the past 21 years, four Oklahomans have won the

prestigious Jack Daniel's World Barbecue Championship, more than any other state. When barbecue competitions became popular a quarter century ago, only three competitions were held annually in Oklahoma. Last year, contestants entered 19 Kansas City Barbeque Society-sanctioned events in the state. The Kansas City Barbeque Society is the world's largest organization of barbecue and grilling enthusiasts.

The largest Oklahoma barbecue cook off is the Bixby BBQ'n Blues Festival. In 2011, more than 199 teams from across the nation competed at Bixby, including several cooks who have claimed the title of World Champion. "Oklahoma cooks are second to none," said Donny Teel of Buffalo's BBQ in Sperry. Teel should know—he competes in nearly 40 barbecue cook offs each year. Teel, who wants the Tulsa area to become a mecca for barbecue, said, "Every weekend we beat each other up, but it makes us that much stronger." Explaining why Oklahoma barbecue is better than in neighboring states, Teel said, "It's like Missouri and Kansas City are one piece of bread and Texas is the

GETTING GRILLED BY WADE CHRISTENSEN

other. All the good stuff is in the middle and that's here
in Oklahoma."

Oklahoma barbecue has influenced other states.
One of the barbeque restaurants that made Kansas City
a barbecue destination is Oklahoma Joe's. If one surfs
the Internet for "Oklahoma barbecue," he is likely to
find Harry's Oklahoma Style Smokehouse in Lomita,
California, or Oklahoma Smokehouse Barbecue in
Eugene, Oregon.

Barbecue has played a major role in the history
of Oklahoma. From pre-statehood days, when the cattle
were rounded up, cowboys and ranchers feasted on the
best barbecued pork and beef. From family reunions to

political gatherings, barbecue meats have been featured to draw large crowds.

In both Oklahoma and Indian territories, beef was barbecued and served at social gatherings such as Juneteenth and July Fourth, church camp meetings, weddings, stomp dances, and on election day. Beef was the meat of choice in early Oklahoma because the Five Civilized Tribes raised mostly cattle. Eventually, Oklahomans developed a palate for a variety of barbecued meats—beef, pork, hot links, chicken, and bologna—served with tomato-based sauce, cole slaw,

A view from a military aircraft from Fort Sill of the long pits at the fairgrounds in Oklahoma City filled with firewood in preparation of the barbecue celebrating the inauguration of Governor Jack Walton in 1923. Bread and other supplies were kept in tents to the left.

baked beans, and potato salad. Added touches included pickles, sliced onions, and hot peppers, with pie for dessert. At statehood, barbecue took center stage. When Charles Haskell became the new state's first governor, a huge barbecue feast was served in a Guthrie park.

The largest Oklahoma barbecue on record was at the inauguration of Governor Jack Walton in 1923. At the old State Fairgrounds in northeast Oklahoma City, Walton and his supporters invited the entire state to a barbecue to celebrate the state's pioneer heritage. Organizers prepared 5,000 chickens, 200 hogs, 200 opossums, 200 sheep, 3,000 rabbits, 1,000 squirrels, 1,000 turkeys, and 500 steers.

Legendary entertainer Henry Gilliland was among fiddlers who vied for the top prize in the fiddlers contest as 160,000 Oklahomans made their way through long lines to partake of the barbecue, beans, and slaw. It was estimated that more than a mile of trenches were dug to cook the tons of meat. Ten thousand gallons of coffee and other beverages were prepared. Thirty string and brass bands performed during the three-day event.

By the 1920s, barbecue restaurants and stands were appearing in large cities and small towns. In 1928, Leroy Vandegrift opened his first Van's Pig

Van's Pig Stand in Norman.

Stand in Wewoka. In Oklahoma City, Norman, and Capitol Hill, Marsh's Pig Stands served "juicy pig" sandwiches on a special bun made by Colonial Bakery. In 1930, the Shawnee Van's Pig Stand opened for business with tender chunks of pork shoulder served with French fries or a twice-baked potato.

In 1941, Alonzo "Slick" Smith established Slick's Bar-B-Que in Muskogee. Slick's trademark was serving brisket with white bread and a chunk of onion on waxed paper. Further east in Sallisaw, Wild Horse Mountain Bar-B-Que held the title as one of the most uniquely-named barbecue restaurants in the state. Bob's Bar-B-Q was located near the end of the runway of the airport in Ada. Many barbecue fans landed in Ada, parked their planes in the grass off the runway, and walked through the neighborhood to Bob's.

In Oklahoma City, Leo Smith began serving barbecue in an old service station. He learned to cook barbecue at age 11 at Ben's Barbecue in Tulsa, a restaurant run by his uncle, Ben Stevenson. Leo was credited with bringing barbecue bologna to Tulsa and Oklahoma City. Leo intrigued his customers by serving homemade banana strawberry cake.

The names of Oklahoma barbecue "joints" are nothing short of special. Many are named for their founders or current proprietors—Bob's, Dan's, Latimer's, Reese's, Reed's, Al's, P.J.'s, Ben's, Pete's, Martin's, or Dink's. Other unique names in Oklahoma barbecue history include Big Buck's Barbecue, Ass Kickin' Bar-B-Que, and the Knotty Pine Bar-B-Q.

Author Michael Wallis wrote in *Oklahoma Today* Magazine:

> *These joints have names like Ethel's, Leo's, and Slick's. They use plastic tableware, serve spongy white bread, and are a far sight less than elegant. And, as every barbecue fan knows, they are reason enough to make your home in Oklahoma.*

Tulsa's Rock 'n' Rib Festival brings music and barbecue together.

OU Heisman Trophy-winning running back Billy Sims has parlayed his fame on the football field to a chain of barbecue restaurants.

Describing a trip to Ethel's 97 Bar-B-Q between Sand Springs and Tulsa, Wallis said, "Hickory smoke scents the air like country incense and lightning bugs blink awake...the juke box is silent, the pinball is quiet, and the pool table sits as still as a graveyard. It's clearly time to eat."

Oklahoma barbecue masters are known for slow cooking and continuous wood smoking of meats over a hickory-wood fire until it is crusty well done. Top-notch barbecue comes only with patience and hard work. Hickory wood long has been a favorite because it produces a smoky and sweet flavor.

Where there is barbecue, there is sauce, and Oklahoma has produced many commercial sauces. Donovan Fred Head developed Head Country Bar-B-Q Sauce in 1945 after serving as a cook in the U.S. Navy during World War II. In 1977, he sold the recipe to his nephew, Danny Head. Head's sauce originally was sold in feed stores until demand outweighed the supply at the Head Country Bar-B-Q Restaurant in Ponca City. Now it is sold worldwide. Head Country teams won the world championship in 1994 and numerous state and regional competitions. Other Oklahoma sauces include Factory's Bar-B-Que made in Okmulgee, Cain's in Tahlequah, Bootleggers in Bartlesville, Hillbilly in Sapulpa, and Latimer's and Martin's in Tulsa.

Anytime Oklahoma celebrates, there usually is a barbecue involved. It was that way when citizens celebrated milestones for the 50th, 75th, and 100th birthdays of the 46th state. Barbecue pork even has made its way into state law. That delicacy is part of the Official State Meal approved by the Oklahoma legislature in 1988.

Barbecue gets involved in politics. Oklahoma Governor Frank Keating and Texas Governor George W. Bush bet on the OU-Texas football game, with the loser hosting a barbecue for the winner. In March, 1997, in Altus, Oklahoma, thousands of fans ate 1,500

Rib Crib has spread its barbecue restaurant franchise beyond state borders. Started by Bret Chandler in an abandoned home in Tulsa in 1992, Rib Crib now operates franchises in seven states in the Heartland and in Florida.

OKLAHOMA BBQ SMOKES THE COMPETITION

pounds of beef brisket donated by a Texas rancher and prepared by Jake's Rib and Hickey's Barbecue, both of Chickasha.

Oklahomans are drawn to annual festivals and barbecue and grilling cook-offs. In 2012, barbecue cooks presented their best ribs and brisket to customers and barbecue fans at such events as the Hog Wild BBQ and Chrome Fest in Chandler, the Smokin' Up a Storm Charity BBQ Challenge in Norman, and the Oklahoma Championship Steak Cook-Off in Tulsa.

Local barbecue and grilling events bring publicity to cities and towns. In June, 2009, *Woman's Day* Magazine called Tecumseh's Barbecue Festival Oklahoma's best BBQ event and one of the top 10 Smokin' BBQ Festivals in the nation. That kind of endorsement and national advertising is worth "big money" to local civic leaders who throw out the welcome mat to teams of barbecuers from around the region.

One historian wrote, "Although people joke about determining the best barbecue joint by the number of pickups and Mercedes in the parking lot, it is no joke that good barbecue draws Oklahomans together to enjoy one of their favorite Southern foods. In the South, barbecue is more than a meal. It's a way of life."

Linda Praytor, right, hosted the barbecue festival in 2009 in Governor Fallin's hometown of Tecumseh.

MADE IN OKLAHOMA

Oklahomans are sometimes surprised to learn that many of the food products on local grocery shelves are produced in the state. Several crops grow well in Oklahoma—nearly half the cropland is planted in wheat. Oklahoma-grown soybeans are used in many common food products such as candy bars and soy sauce. Vast orchards produce a variety of fresh fruits. Four shelling plants in Oklahoma handle most of the state's crop of Spanish peanuts. Oklahoma is one of only 11 states that produce pecans. A substantial part of the state economy is tied to manufacturing of processed foods.

Oklahoma-grown fruits of many kinds make incredible fruit salads and appetizer trays.

For many years, fairs and festivals have highlighted locally-produced products. The largest trade show giving Oklahoma food producers the opportunity to connect with potential customers is at the Tulsa State Fair. The Market Development Division of the Oklahoma Department of Agriculture, Food, & Forestry (ODAFF) established the Made in Oklahoma (MIO) program to promote brand awareness, trade, and consumer loyalty for Oklahoma food products.

GETTING GRILLED BY WADE CHRISTENSEN

A website, www.madeinoklahoma.net, was created to give consumers a link to an online shopping mall, listing companies enrolled in the MIO program. The website also features a listing of farmers' markets and retailers that carry made-in-Oklahoma products.

Wholesale trade shows provide MIO companies a chance to exhibit their products to retailers in two- or three-day exhibits each July at the Wholesale Gift Show, a critical time when wholesale buyers are placing large orders for the holiday season. ODAFF also builds relationships with retail grocery stores to host in-store demonstrations. The Oklahoma Gift Basket Directory is published by the MIO program and highlights companies that produce baskets of products made in Oklahoma.

Recently, Oklahoma State University teamed with the Robert M. Kerr Food & Agricultural Products Center for a Made in Oklahoma Month. Students and faculty went to the OSU Student Union to taste products made in Oklahoma. Representatives of Oklahoma companies emphasized the impact of Oklahoma-produced food, including the fact that Lopez Foods distributed sausage patties and meat, and The Bama Companies, famous for its pies, provided biscuits for McDonald's in Oklahoma and surrounding states.

In April, 2012, Governor Mary Fallin and First Gentleman Wade Christensen kicked off the annual Made in Oklahoma Month, an annual celebration inaugurated by Governor Frank Keating in 2001, by enjoying several dishes made with food products made in Oklahoma. The recipes were created by David Henry with The Coach House Restaurant in Oklahoma City and included ingredients from five MIO companies—Shawnee Milling Company, JC Potter Sausage Company, Braum's Ice Cream and Dairy Stores, Lopez Foods, and Hiland Dairy.

Recipes created by David Henry for the 2012 Made in Oklahoma celebration

Breakfast Bites

ONE (SIX-OUNCE) PACKAGE SHAWNEE
MILLS BUTTERMILK PANCAKE MIX
8 OUNCES REGULAR JC POTTER SAUSAGE
3 OUNCES SHREDDED PEPPER JACK CHEESE
1 EGG
¼ CUP HILAND OR BRAUM'S MILK

In a mixing bowl, stir together all the ingredients and shape into one-inch balls. Bake for 15 minutes at 375 degrees. Makes 24 (one ounce) bites.

Firecracker Spoon Bread

1 ¾ CUPS SHAWNEE MILLS WHITE CORN MEAL
1 TABLESPOON BAKING POWDER
1 TEASPOON BAKING SODA
2 EGGS
2 ¼ CUP HILAND OR BRAUM'S BUTTERMILK
1 PACKAGE FROZEN PRE-COOKED COUNTRY
     COUSIN SAUSAGE THAWED AND FINELY CUT
1 CUP FROZEN SWEET CORN
¼ CUP FINELY DICED RED PEPPER
1 TABLESPOON RINSED AND CHOPPED PARSLEY
2 TABLESPOONS FINELY DICED JALAPENO
8 OUNCES SHREDDED SHARP CHEESE

Place seasoned skillet in 350 degree oven. In a bowl, combine white corn meal, baking powder, baking soda, eggs, and buttermilk to make the batter. Add sausage, sweet corn, diced red pepper, parsley, jalapeno, and shredded cheese.

Remove skillet from oven and fill with mixture. Bake for 25-30 minutes or until toothpick when inserted still has a bit of the batter on it when removed. Let sit for 5-10 minutes before serving.

Shortbread Cookies
with **Strawberries**

SHORTBREAD INGREDIENTS:
7 OUNCES HILAND OR BRAUM'S BUTTER
5 ¼ OUNCE POWDERED SUGAR
4 EGG YOLKS
1 WHOLE EGG
PINCH OF SALT
11 OUNCES WHOLE WHEAT FLOUR

FILLING/TOPPING INGREDIENTS:
16 LARGE STRAWBERRIES
¼ CUP VANILLA-INFUSED SUGAR
2 TABLESPOONS GARDEN CLUB STRAWBERRY JAM
HILAND WHIPPING CREAM, WHIPPED

Preheat oven to 350 degrees. Cream together butter and powdered sugar. Beat in egg yolks and one whole egg.

Combine wet mixture with dry ingredients and stir together until blended. Divide batter into one-ounce balls, pat flat by hand, and place on a cookie sheet. Bake 15 minutes or until brown.

Filling: Cut sixteen large strawberries lengthwise into eight small strips per berry. Toss with one-fourth cup of vanilla-infused sugar* and two tablespoons of Garden Club Strawberry Jam and let sit for one hour. Whip one pint of Hiland whipping cream for topping.

Place one cookie on plate, top with a large spoon of strawberry mixture, a dollop of whipped cream and another cookie. Garnish with a sprig of mint, if desired, and enjoy!

*Vanilla-infused sugar can be made by adding dried vanilla bean pods to sugar. Store mixture in a sealed container; when ready to use, discard the vanilla bean pods.

MADE IN OKLAHOMA COALITION

In 2000, several Oklahoma food manufacturers met to discuss ways to work together to increase sales of their products. The idea was to pool resources to fund a marketing campaign. Their goal was to make consumers aware of the great quality and diversity of Oklahoma-made food product brands.

As a result of the discussions, the Made in Oklahoma (MIO) Coalition was born. Membership is limited to companies that produce Oklahoma food or agricultural products. Companies who are members of the MIO Coalition employ more than 20,000 workers with an annual payroll of nearly $800-million. Annual sales of Oklahoma food brands now exceed $3-billion, 85 percent of which is exported to other states and countries.

MADE IN OKLAHOMA

SHARING **THE GREAT TASTE** OF LIFE FOR

100 YEARS

GRIFFINS**100**.COM

Watonga cheese aging. More than 60 kinds of cheese are made by Watonga Cheese, an idea that became a reality in 1940. Cheese tasting and a food contest are a part of the annual Watonga Cheese Festival.

MIO Companies

Company	Category
AdvancePierre Foods	Meats
Bar-S Foods Company	Meats
Big Mike's Homestyle Salsa, LLC	Canned
Billy Sims BBQ	Condiments, Sauces
Braum's Ice Cream and Dairy Stores	Dairy
Charlie Bean Coffee	Beverages
Chef's Requested Foods	Meats
Clements Foods Company	Condiments, Sauces
Cusack Meats	Meats
Daddy Hinkle's	Herbs, Spices
Field's Pies	Desserts
From the Woods LLC	Condiments, Sauces
Griffin Foods Company	Breakfast
Head Country	Condiments, Sauces
Henderson Coffee Corporation	Beverages
Hiland Dairy	Dairy
Iron Starr BBQ Sauce	Condiments, Sauces
JC Potter Sausage Company	Meats
Ken's Bakery	Desserts
Kreb's Brewing Company	Beverages
La Baguette	Baking
Lopez Foods	Meats
My Bigmama's Kitchen	Desserts
Natural Water Company, LLC	Beverages
Neighbors Coffee	Beverages
O'Steen Meat Specialties	Meats
OK Foods	Meats
Premium Natural Beef	Meats
Ralph's Packing Company	Meats
Schwab & Company	Meats
Serapio's Tortillas	Baked products
Shawnee Milling Company	Breakfast
Split T Hickory Sauce LLC	Condiments, Sauces
Suan's Foods Inc.	Condiments, Sauces
The Bama Companies, Inc.	Baking
The Original Chili Bowl	Main Meal Entrees
Twin Foods, Inc.	Canned
Value Added Products	Baking
Van's Pig Stands BBQ Sauce	Condiments, Sauces
Vinyard Fruit & Vegetable Company	Fruits and vegetables

OKLAHOMA FOOD COOPERATIVE

The Oklahoma Food Cooperative (OFC) links consumers with Oklahoma-made products. Their website offers more than 4,000 items each month. As an "online farmers market," the OFC brings together producers and customers in the same organization to discover unique and authentic regional tastes of Oklahoma. OFC brings willing buyers in contact with willing sellers. For an annual fee to join the co-op, producers can sell, and customers can buy everything from water from Oklahoma artesian wells, wholegrain breads from a home bakery north of Edmond, pound cakes and cookies from commercial small-town bakeries, homemade salsa from a Stillwater Mexican restaurant owner, and yogurt cheese from a dairy at Helena.

Oklahoma strawberries are celebrated at the Stilwell Strawberry Festival each year. Live music, a carnival, and the crowning of the Stilwell Strawberry Festival queen complement a large array of foods made from strawberries.

GETTING GRILLED BY WADE CHRISTENSEN

Some of the past royalty of the McLoud Blackberry Festival held since the 1940s to celebrate the end of the harvest season.

The huckleberry festival at Jay features a car show, carnival, parade, and huckleberry pancakes, and many more dishes made from huckleberries.

Porter holds an annual festival that features hundreds of food dishes and products made from Oklahoma peaches. More than 15,000 people attended the 45th annual Porter Peach Festival in 2012. Peach tea and peach ice cream were some of the foods vendors used to attract crowds.

The largest annual Oklahoma watermelon festival is at Rush Springs. The festival has been held each summer continuously since 1948. Up to 30,000 people are served more than 50,000 pounds of watermelon purchased from area growers.

INDEX

GETTING GRILLED BY WADE CHRISTENSEN